❦❦❦

A New Heart...
a New Start

❦❦❦

Discovering
the Promise of
Restoration

❦❦❦

A Devotional Daybook

by Neva Coyle

🍒🍒🍒

A New Heart... a New Start

🍒🍒🍒

Discovering
the Promise of
Restoration

🍒🍒🍒

BETHANY HOUSE PUBLISHERS
MINNEAPOLIS, MINNESOTA 55438

Published by Bethany House Publishers
A Ministry of Bethany Fellowship, Inc.
6820 Auto Club Road, Minneapolis, Minnesota 55438

Printed in the United States of America

Library of Congress Cataloging-in-Publication Data

Coyle, Neva, 1943–
    A new heart—a new start / Neva Coyle.
       p. cm. — (A Devotional daybook)

    1. Devotional exercises. 2. Bible. O.T. Psalms LI—Meditations.
3. David, King of Israel—Meditations.
I. Title. II. Series: Coyle, Neva, 1943–   Devotional daybook.
BV4832.2.C68   1992
242'.2—dc20   92–30227
ISBN 1–55661–277–X   CIP

To Janet

NEVA COYLE is Founder of Overeaters Victorious and President of Neva Coyle Ministries. Her ministry is enhanced by her bestselling books, tapes, and teaching seminars. Neva and her husband make their home in California.

She may be contacted at:

P.O. Box 2330
Orange, CA 92669

Preface

IN THE COURSE OF NORMAL LIFE there are times, perhaps brought on by trying circumstances, when each of us would like to throw up our hands and cry to God for a chance to start over.

Many of us have felt frustration for our failures at making positive changes in our lives. Many of us experience a sense of defeat when trying to dig out of emotional pits we have made by giving too much of ourselves in unhealthy relationships, or because we have made foolish decisions. Some of us have simply grown tired of the conflict between worldliness and godliness. Others feel downcast because of illness or personal crisis. And there are those who have given in to temptation and have taken a serious fall that has crippled their relationship with Jesus Christ. Each of these difficulties can cause our relationship with God to seem cold and stale.

There are others, too, who feel the need of a fresh start. I am thinking of the times when we strive hard for a long time to make something "good" happen only to find that circumstances keep pushing the goal just beyond our fingertips. Even those who have been doing God's will, actively doing God's work for a long time, can suddenly find their spiritual lives are less exciting and fulfilling than they were—wasn't it just a few months ago?

There are some who can identify with a "creeping" crisis— the crisis that crept up so quietly it seemed to suddenly appear. Many people can identify with struggles that occur on more than one front—marriage, finances, job, and church. If we would but take the time to ask those right around us in our churches and even our homes, we would find many who are feeling that their spiritual anchors have come loose and that they are drifting—feeling aimless with no direction or goal. And what's worse, many really don't know what to do about it.

If you can identify with any of these situations I've just mentioned, and you could use new freshness, a new beginning, then this is the book for you. Using the experience and prayer of David found in Psalm 51 as a basis for devotional study— day by day—you can experience not only a new start but a new heart.

David knew what it was to do what God had asked him to do, and still to have everything go wrong. He had been anointed king only to be later pursued like a criminal. He had hidden himself for safety before finally taking on the responsibility of king. He had quite a bit of crises, and he had grown weary. Then in a weak moment he yielded to the temptation of his own sexual desire for another man's wife—and entered a time of deception, manipulation, and finally murder to cover his failure.

David's moral failure is not really where the story ends, but where it begins—with a new start and a new heart. Your circumstance is not the end: It can be the beginning. Let these days with this book be your new start. You too can experience the creation of a new heart.

If you are currently enjoying a rich, satisfying relationship with Christ, this book will serve to deepen your relationship. Perhaps you are presently disillusioned with your life—maybe even yourself—and are ready to make a break with unhappiness, struggle, and defeat. This book will help you find the path out of self-centered living and into the freedom of Christ-centered living. To do this we will discover hidden traps of self-motivation, and turn these into chances for becoming Christ-motivated.

The Bible is the well containing the living water of God's Word, and so it is through His Word, eternal and unchanging, that we will build a more vital relationship with our living Lord. My goal is to help you rediscover how God's Word can become the source of new life as you spend time reading and applying it to your life and your present situation.

In this study, we will walk with David through a dire moment, when he faced a crisis of spiritual surrender. Let the areas of your life that are yet unsurrendered be exposed to the fresh healing touch of God's Word. David's personal failures were not unlike various situations we face today. We will take a close look at this "man after God's own heart" and how he pressed through failure and what seemed to be the end of God's dealings with him—to a higher, newer place in spirit. His thoughts and prayers at this crucial time in his life give us words and issues to consider. May each of us learn from them our own fight of faith.

The object of this study is to help you learn how surrendering yourself to Christ will give a new heart—that is, a new inclination and new motivation to live a life set apart for God. You will not only find a new freedom but you will encounter His grace at a depth you may never have known before. I recommend you read Psalm 51 often, perhaps in different versions of the Bible. I believe this will add deeper insight to your study. As a result, I know that you will take a giant step in personal growth toward a new heart—the new start you have been wanting through learning total surrender.

God bless you as you begin!

Contents

How to Use This Book

THIS DEVOTIONAL STUDY is designed to fit easily into a busy schedule. It is divided into six sections, with five entries in each section. If an entry is read each day, it will take just thirty days to complete the book. Take a few minutes each day to read the suggested scripture and accompanying thought. The questions at the end of each entry will guide your focus on a personal application of the scripture selection. Writing your own response in the space after questions will help you better establish the scriptural truths in your life.

If the book is used in a group study, members should study the five entries of a section during the week and then meet as a group to discuss the material. In this way the book will take six weeks to complete, or longer depending on the needs of the group. It also is easily adaptable to a women's ministry group that is already established, or a Sunday school class.

If you are using this material in a group study, suggested guidelines and discussion questions are included at the end of the book for the use of the leader.

Section I

Mercy

*H*ave mercy on me, O God,
  according to your unfailing love;
according to your great compassion
  blot out my transgressions.
Wash away all my iniquity
  and cleanse me from my sin.
For I know my transgressions,
  and my sin is always before me.
Against you, you only, have I sinned
  and done what is evil in your sight,
so that you are proved right when you speak
  and justified when you judge.
Surely I was sinful at birth,
  sinful from the time my mother conceived me.
Surely you desire truth in the inner parts;
  you teach me wisdom in the inmost place.
Cleanse me with hyssop, and I will be clean;
  wash me, and I will be whiter than snow.
Let me hear joy and gladness;
  let the bones you have crushed rejoice.
Hide your face from my sins
  and blot out all my iniquity.
Create in me a clean heart, O God,
  and renew a steadfast spirit within me.
Do not cast me from your presence
  or take your Holy Spirit from me.
Restore to me the joy of your salvation
  and grant me a willing spirit, to sustain me.
Then I will teach transgressors your ways,
  and sinners will turn back to you.
Save me from bloodguilt, O God,
  the God who saves me,
  and my tongue will sing of your righteousness.
O Lord, open my lips,
  and my mouth will declare your praise.
You do not delight in sacrifice, or I would bring it;
  you do not take pleasure in burnt offerings.
The sacrifices of God are a broken spirit;
  a broken and contrite heart,
  O God, you will not despise.
In your good pleasure make Zion prosper;
  build up the walls of Jerusalem.
Then there will be righteous sacrifices,
  whole burnt offerings to delight you;
  then bulls will be offered on your altar.

PSALM 51

16

HAVE YOU EVER ASKED yourself what chance you would have without God's mercy? Did you ever wonder what God would be like if He were merciless instead of merciful? Or has something of His mercy and compassion escaped you still?

Mercy adds a dimension to our relationship with God that goes even deeper than the knowledge that we are forgiven. Receiving God's forgiveness is absolutely important when admitting the wrong we have done—but mercy reaches out to the misery we feel because of our failings.

We experience misery, not only as a result of our own sin, but because the sin of others hurts us, too. Misery grips us because of oppressions and compulsions we can't seem to conquer, or because of a bad attitude of depression we can't overcome.

Mercy is a vast part of God's eternal character, which is boundless and life-saving. It is the character quality of God that noticed our need for salvation, and it is with a heart of mercy that He encourages us to repent, with the promise of full forgiveness.

Forgiveness cleanses us from moral guilt; mercy helps us recover from pain.

In this first part, we will look at five reflections about mercy:

1. God is by nature a merciful God.
2. People can be merciless.
3. Our lives can be victimized by mercy killers, until we "root them out."
4. Simple acts of lovingkindness are daily expressions of mercy.
5. We can rely on the tender mercies of God.

Chapter
· 1 ·

Mercy

"Have mercy on me, O God, according to your unfailing love; according to your great compassion blot out my transgressions."

Psalm 51:1

"For the Lord your God is a merciful God."

Deuteronomy 4:31

DAVID WAS WELL-ACQUAINTED with God's mercy, and had even demonstrated it in his actions. At his finest hour, he had shown himself to be a man of great self-control. When the chance to kill Saul, his enemy, was within David's power and there was every understandable reason to do so—David chose to be merciful.

Yet . . . with his soldiers off to war, and unable to rest on a spring evening, David took a stroll on his upper porch and saw Bathsheba. Challenge and hardship had served to make him stronger; restlessness and the beauty of this woman revealed his weakness.

This was David's worst hour, in which he utterly failed God. Eventually, he would abuse his kingly power, deceive one of his best soldiers, and have him murdered.

David, the man after God's own heart, though acquainted with God's protective and delivering mercy, mercilessly destroyed a man's life—and very nearly his own.

How ironic—and how human—it seems that the man who showed no mercy cried out for God's mercy: "Have mercy on me, O God . . ." David cried. Not because of what he thought he deserved, but because of the God he knew.

There are times in the life of every one of us when only God's mercy will help. These times may be preceded by a severe fall in our walk with God and in the standard of conduct we hold for ourselves, but not always. Sometimes we are beaten by circumstances; or job and family pressures become unbearable; or we suffer abuse at the hands of another. For each of us there are times when we simply cannot take it any longer. We are miserable, wounded, and defeated.

The truth is, we are all in need of God's mercy—all of the time, not just when we know we need it. And the good news is that it is available for us.

Are you hoping for an experience that goes beyond the assurance of God's forgiveness? His mercy is not something we deserve, not something we can earn. It's not even available because of any love we have for Him, but because of His love for us!

———

To get a taste of this mercy write your own personalized version of the following verse:

"For God so loved the world that he gave his one and only Son, that whoever believes in him shall not perish but have eternal life" (John 3:16).

You may want to start like this: For God so loved _(your name here)_ that he . . .

Do the same with this verse:

> "This is love: not that we loved God, but that he loved us and sent his Son as an atoning sacrifice for our sins" (1 John 4:10).

This is love: not that _____(your name here)_____ loved God, but that he loved _____(your name here)_____ and . . .

When you think of the above verses, with your name inserted, what impression of God's mercy do you have?

If you were more aware of God's mercy and its ready availability for you, what fear, goal, or hope would you be more willing to face honestly in prayer?

When you read the above verses personalized, do you find your thoughts today more in line with God's promises, or more in opposition to them? Why?

Because accepting God's mercy is essential to giving you a new start, what specific areas of your life do you need to have touched with His mercy?

Chapter · 2 ·

Merciless

"Who may ascend the hill of the Lord? Who may stand in his holy place? He who has clean hands and a pure heart, who does not lift up his soul to an idol or swear by what is false."

Psalm 24:3

"I cry aloud to the Lord; I lift up my voice to the Lord for mercy. I pour out my complaint before him; before him I tell my trouble. When my spirit grows faint within me, it is you who know my way. In the path where I walk men have hidden a snare for me. Look to my right and see; no one is concerned for me. I have no refuge; no one cares for my life."

Psalm 142:1–4

IT'S NOT EVERY DAY that someone like David comes along. He was known as the man "after God's own heart," and he was chosen to be king while just a youth and a mere shepherd. He was schooled as a young harpist in obedience and patience. His faith was challenged as a boy-warrior and strengthened with victory. David was blessed in the trusted friendship of Saul's son Jonathan but had his trust in the Lord tested as he fled for "safety" to the very midst of Israel's enemies.

Think about it: David was superb! No other man had such insight into spiritual truth, or the privilege of such intimacy in worship. He enjoyed a father-and-son relationship with God unequaled in his day—and long before Christ opened the way for all of us.

Yet there was a dark corner of his personality that David had not given to the Lord. Sadly, that unsanctified corner corrupted every other area of his heart and life. Did he recover fully what his life would have been without his devastating mistakes? How can we ever know for sure?

His area of weakness clearly changed the course of his life. This man who had experienced God's mercy for himself withheld it from another.

Getting another man's wife pregnant in his absence was terrible enough. But see the whole picture: Uriah was out fighting David's battle. To save himself, David entered wholeheartedly into deception. David called Uriah home, pretending to want his opinion on the progress of the war. It was a natural set-up. Uriah would sleep with his wife and David would cover his shameful act. The plan didn't work, because Uriah had a sense of personal ethics, and he would not allow himself such pleasure while his men were still engaging in battle. Imagine the mixture of panic, shame, guilt, and even jealousy that David might have felt.

And so David let fear of exposure turn him to thoughts of murder. He caused Uriah's soldiers to betray him, and then took Bathsheba as his own. He got what he wanted, but his soul had paid a heavy price.

David clearly wanted God's will but he had his own hidden motives as well.

The psalms above were written before David ever saw Bathsheba on that spring evening and so we know that David was fully acquainted with God's mercy. And yet, because he had received mercy, it did not guarantee that he would show it toward another.

What about you? Have you experienced God's mercy? Could you have survived and progressed this far in your spiritual life without it?

Name someone to whom you have shown mercy.

Name someone who needed mercy from you, and you withheld it.

How is God impressing on you your need to be more merciful?

If you are determined to show more mercy, how will the Lord need to help you in certain relationships?

While God desires that we show mercy toward one another, His mercy toward us is not dependent upon it. Simply stated, His mercy is not patterned after ours, but ours must be patterned after His.

Later, David writes, "The Lord has heard my cry for mercy; the Lord accepts my prayer" (see Psalm 6). Perhaps you have shown a lack of mercy toward another. Is it a pattern in your life that you have not recognized before? Ask God to help you to be more merciful toward the people you meet today.

"Be merciful, just as your Father is merciful."
Luke 6:36

"MERCY KILLERS" are everywhere. They can become such a part of your daily life that you won't even realize it until the damage is done. Mercy killers are the secret *attitudes* that kill gentleness, generosity, goodwill.

Perhaps you've noticed the dead feelings you get when someone says your family, business, or church should be run differently.

You witnessed a mercy killing when your friend gossiped about a neighbor or when Aunt Jane refused to come to a dinner party because Uncle Harold's wife was also invited.

Perhaps you have noticed a numbness creeping up inside you after many days or months of caring for a sick child or an elderly parent. Their needs and demands seem to wear you out and rub your temper thin.

Perhaps you may have participated in a mercy killing or committed one all by yourself.

Think about it. Have you criticized someone who could have used your support? Did you do it because they don't do things your way? Did you pass on a doubt about someone's character simply because you don't understand them? Did you leave a false impression that could be interpreted as truth?

Have you secretly rejoiced when someone of whom you are jealous suffers? Did you look the other way when someone was disappointed and needed encouragement, telling yourself it was none of your business? Do you remember a frosty feeling that settled in your heart when you listened without emotion while someone tried to share their pain with you?

If you can answer yes to any of these questions, you have been a victim or a perpetrator of a mercy killing. Somehow our ability to be merciful has been seriously wounded.

But criticism, gossip, and jealously are not the only mercy killers. In addition we can list doubt, self-centeredness, lies, self-righteousness, stubbornness, and judgmentalism.

As you can see, we can be both victim and "killer." Little by little we can experience loss of compassion and care. We cut ourselves off from others emotionally and then wonder at the isolation we feel.

Adults who were abused as children are one example of victims of mercy killings. Emotional detachment at the time of the abuse helped them survive—for the moment. But later, many struggle with a lack of ability to feel healthy affection for others. Those who were molested as children often report negative reactions to wholesome, loving touch as adults. These may discover that the "tender shoot" that was meant to grow into mercy has withered within.

It is never hopeless, never too late. We can be changed. While the death of mercy may be traced to its roots—even understood—it does not have to be permanent. Through Jesus Christ anyone may discover how to feel again. Our wonderful merciful Savior can reach even your deepest, secret scars and heal them. Through His miraculous touch you and I can be made whole.

What does this mean? Only by opening yourself to His touch, His life can make us merciful, just as our Father is merciful.

Today, why not make this turning point in your life: Ask God to return to you a capacity for mercy. Let the following questions lead you to recognize your need, then turn to Him for mercy.

———

What type of misery have you witnessed that grips you emotionally to the point of wanting to do something to bring relief?

What type of misery do you see around you that you know is there but does not move you at all?

What does it mean if you are moved to help one miserable person and not another?

How have you had your own misery relieved by another's act of mercy?

What "mercy killers" are you most aware of now?

What is God impressing on you about mercy?

Spend time meditating on your desire to be more merciful.

Chapter
· 4 ·

Lovingkindness

"Thy lovingkindness is better than life."
Psalm 63:3, KJV

WITHOUT A WORD she approached the clear plastic IV bags that hung above my head and inspected the tubing. This nurse had just come on duty, and I was a total stranger to her, having come from surgery that morning.

"What time is it?" I asked.

"A little after three," she replied.

"Can I have something for pain?"

"I'll check," she said. Then she left my room.

A little later she returned and, without a word, checked the tubing and solution level.

"Can I have something for pain?" I repeated.

"You asked me only ten minutes ago. I said I'll check and I will," she said with mild irritation in her voice and no eye contact as she took hold of the tubing where the needle was inserted in my arm.

Without thinking I grabbed her hand and suddenly had her full attention. "I'm a real person inside here," I said, surprised at my own boldness. "Please treat me like a real person. Pain robs you of all sense of time. All I realize is pain."

She stiffened and left the room. Within seconds she was back, her eyes moist and her voice soft. "Can you wait another twenty or thirty minutes? Then I can give you a shot." She handed me her watch. "This will help you mark the time." She straightened my covers and sat beside me on the bed.

"I'm sorry about—well, before." Looking straight into my eyes she continued, "May I sit here and talk, until it's time for your shot? Would you like a backrub?"

Even those who are professional mercy-givers sometimes fail at their profession.

Most of us have counted on someone for mercy—a teacher or an employer, only to have them fail us. Many have experienced unmerciful parents. They do the right things, perform the right tasks, and say the right phrases, but, like my nurse, sometimes their actions are unmerciful—empty.

God is never like that. For Him mercy is not a profession. It is His character. It's not a part of His "job description." It is His very nature, always woven through with lovingkindness.

Can you identify times when others have failed to show you mercy? How have those times encouraged you to treat others in the same way? We may not see where we are unmerciful until we compare ourselves with His pattern of mercy. Only then do we see our need to change.

Why does such a merciful God continue to extend to us, the unloving, His matchless mercy? I believe it's because He is confident we can change. We cannot change ourselves. But His power working through our obedient attitudes changes us. Can you identify a merciless act that you have done?

What attitudes were behind it? If we are to make a fresh start, we need to walk like David did into a deeper experience of God's mercy.

Read the words of Psalm 86:1–5:

"Hear, O LORD, and answer me,
for I am poor and needy.
Guard my life, for I am devoted to you.
You are my God, save your servant
who trusts in You.
Have mercy on me, O LORD,
for I call to you all day long,
Bring joy to your servant,

for to you, O LORD,
I lift up my soul.
You are forgiving and good, O LORD,
   abounding in love to all who call to you."

If you were to pray this prayer for yourself, asking God to save you from performing merciless acts, what difference would you expect to see in your life? In your attitudes to others?

What is God impressing on you about His lovingkindness?

What do you need to confess concerning your own hurts because of unloving actions against you?

Can you think of someone who can use lovingkindness today?

Think of a way to express an act of lovingkindness to that person.

Tender
Mercies

*"Have mercy on me, O God, according to your unfailing
love; according to your great compassion."*

Psalm 51:1

THE KEY TO A FRESH START comes as we explore the
deeper level of relationship with God that is available to us.
David knew, and reveals to us three levels.

Mercy—the evidence of God's total authority.

Mercy is the act of relieving pain or pressure in another's
life. It may be that we suspend a penalty—not giving a person
what he deserves, and pardoning instead. Mercy is what we
receive when we accept Jesus Christ as our personal Savior.
When we confess our sins, He forgives us. We no longer have
to fear getting what we deserve because of our sins—we have
received mercy.

At the first level of our relationship with God we experience salvation.

Lovingkindness—the evidence of God's love *for* us.

God's love is unfailing. Nothing you have done or ever
will do can cause it to crumble. Though you may reject God's
love, He will not reject you. His love is permanent and noth-

ing you have ever done or will ever do can make it go away. It is unchanging, it will never, never be any different. God's love does not flow in and out like the tide. It is eternal, and it will outlast everything that we consider permanent—the world, the universe . . .

God's unfailing love is the level at which He performs in our behalf—"I will perform that which concerns you" (Psalm 138:8). While lovingkindness is extended, it does not really require anything more than benevolence or good wishes on the part of the giver. It simply means that the giver has feelings for the receiver.

It is because of God's lovingkindness that we depend on this: He is there *for* us.

At this level of relationship we can and do know God as benefactor. He answers our prayers out of His lovingkindness. It is solid, unfailing, and we can always count on His love.

Compassion—the evidence of His commitment to be involved *with* us.

Because of His compassion, we are convinced that God desires to feel *with* us.

"For we do not have a high priest who is unable to sympathize with our weaknesses, but we have one who has been tempted in every way, just as we are—yet was without sin" (Hebrews 4:15).

And: "I no longer call you servants . . . I have called you friends" (John 15:15).

Jesus came down to our level. He felt what we feel, He struggled with our difficulties. He fought the same battles we fight, and overcame the same fears we face. He even bore our sins.

Mercy shows God's powerful authority, lovingkindness lets us observe His grace and compassion, lets us experience it. It reveals His tenderness toward us. None of this is dependent on us—we have not forced God to be any of these things. God's character is the way He is, and He is offering to us *himself*.

He offers to us His matchless mercy, His unfailing love, and His compassion. Today, He wants you to know that He is not only there *for* you—He is there *with* you.

He wants you to depend on Him as your benefactor. And—as if this weren't enough—He extends to you His hand, to walk with you as friend. Is it hard for you to accept this? Why settle for mercy and lovingkindness only, when you can also have His friendship—friendship that is guaranteed to last into eternity?

There is no purchase necessary—He paid the entire price! No down-payment—the account is paid in full! No salesman will call—this is a personal relationship! This is a no-risk offer—He took all the risks. What have you got to lose?

———

Can you think of the reasons we reject His offer of mercy?

What are the consequences?

What are some reasons we reject His offer of lovingkindness?

What are the consequences?

Are you ready to accept His offer of friendship? Write out your acceptance.

What results can you expect?

Section II

Encounter With
Power

Blot out my transgressions.
Wash away all my iniquity
    and cleanse me from my sin.
For I know my transgressions,
    and my sin is always before me.
Against you, you only, have I sinned
    and done what is evil in your sight,
so that you are proved right when you speak
    and justified when you judge.
Surely I was sinful at birth,
    sinful from the time my mother conceived me.

PSALM 51:1–5

"I COULDN'T RESIST."
   "I can't help myself when it comes to. . . ."
   "It's one of my weaknesses."
   Do you recognize any of these statements? Acting like victims, giving in without resistance means we are not really dealing with our weaknesses—but giving in to our strongholds. These are not the areas in which we are powerless—but powerful. Giving in only helps us to maintain our selfish interests while we feign helplessness.
   In this second part of our devotional study, we will look at several power points and learn to use them to our good and for our growth instead of to our selfish advantage:

1. The power of sin and self.
2. The power of confession.
3. The power of the past.
4. The power of repentance.
5. Truth, not excuses.

Chapter · 6 ·

The Power of Sin and Self

"Blot out my transgressions."

Psalm 57:1

FOUR SIMPLE WORDS tell an entire story.

The once-powerful king admits he is powerless. He has encountered the power of sin and self—and lost.

David dug his way into an emotional and spiritual pit, and could not get out.

What about you? Don't you wish your record was perfect? Have you, like David, gotten in over your head? Do you sometimes feel like you are drowning in a sea of guilt and self-loathing? It may not be a matter of sin and guilt for you. It may be that you are just too tired to go on carrying the load you have been bearing far too long.

Maybe you filter every opportunity to serve Jesus through past sin, and feel unworthy. Or perhaps you filter every opportunity to trust Him through past failure, and fail again.

Maybe you have thought "out of sight, out of mind," and made efforts to forget, when what you have really needed is for God to remove the guilt and shame.

A new time, a new place, you thought as you packed up and moved away from your problems. But has running really been the answer? Somehow we manage to bring a piece of the past with us. . . .

Believe it or not, life can change. You can change. You can be free to begin anew—start over.

Let's face it, each of us has something in our past we are ashamed of. Mistakes, failures, and regret are at the very least a small part of every life. Discouragement, weariness, and burnout characterize many others.

Are you feeling overwhelmed? Is your joy and peace threatened? Is your energy being drained?

David was overwhelmed: "Like a burden too heavy to bear," he called it (Psalm 38:4).

If you could write the same verse (Psalm 38:4) what would you say?

I am overwhelmed by _____ , like a burden too heavy to bear.

Fortunately, like David, our story need not end here.

In four simple words, David reveals five important facts:

"Blot out *my* transgressions." By accepting past mistakes, he recognized his own humanity with its vulnerability. He also accepted the responsibility for those mistakes.

By accepting his mistakes, he also recognized his powerlessness to do anything about the consequences.

By exposing his transgressions, he exposes himself.

By asking God to blot them out, he recognizes that God alone has the power to deal with sinful behaviors and selfishness.

He confesses the reality that his only hope for restoration is in God's ability—alone.

David needed God because of his sin: What is *your* most pressing need?

If you were convinced of the five important factors above, how would your prayers about your need change?

If you were fully convinced of God's willingness to use His power to help you "blot out" your sins and shortcomings, how would it change the way you approach Him?

Why forgo the freedom His forgiveness and power offer?

Why put off the freedom of a fresh start one moment longer?

Make this the moment of decision to give God that which is threatening to overwhelm you. Don't hesitate. You approach a wonderful and loving God. He is waiting for you to respond to Him—He is ready to respond to you.

Keep in mind your need *and* God's power and His mercy.

Think of God, saying the following: (Fill in the blanks with what you think God would say to you.)
"Come. Discover my _____."
"Accept my _____."
"Experience my _____."

Only God has the power to cut through all the bindings of the past. Only He can restore the joy of a new start. What's more, you can count on Him—*if you will.*

Tell Him anything you need to tell Him.

Can you settle it in your mind—that He hears you?

Chapter · 7 ·

The Power of Confession

"If we confess our sins, he is faithful and just and will forgive us our sins."

1 John 1:9

Then Joshua said to Achan, "My son, give glory to the Lord, the God of Israel, and give him the praise. Tell me what you have done; do not hide it from me."
Achan replied, "It is true! I have sinned against the Lord, the God of Israel. This is what I have done: When I saw in the plunder a beautiful robe from Babylonia, two hundred shekels of silver, and a wedge of gold weighing fifty shekels, I coveted them and took them. They are hidden in the ground inside my tent, and the silver underneath." So Joshua sent messengers, and they ran to the tent, and there it was, hidden in his tent, with the silver underneath.

Joshua 7:19–21

A YOUNG SOLDIER, still feeling the power of victory, met a temptation too great to resist. The warrior fell, not in battle—but in his heart.

Come forth, he was told. Confess. How many of us would have been as forthright?

We approach God sometimes with a certain false innocence, and while we acknowledge our involvement, we are reluctant to *confess* our guilt. When mere acknowledgment doesn't seem to work, and peace and forgiveness are still evasive, we move in a little closer and *admit* a relationship with sin. For example, we may admit—under the pressure of conviction—that while we flirt with the world, we are not under its influence. We admit the act, but try to remain innocent.

Eventually, like Achan, we can no longer hide. It is time to tell the truth about not only our sin, but our guilt. It is time to *confess*, and like David we pray:

"Against you, you only, have I sinned and done what is evil in your sight, so that you are proved right when you speak and justified when you judge" (Psalm 51:4).

The words of Ezra 9:6 express how we feel:

"O my God, I am too ashamed and disgraced to lift up my face to you, my God, because our sins are higher than our heads and our guilt has reached to the heavens."

The admission of our sin is not complete with the admission of our guilt. Only then can we begin to experience the relief of God's merciful forgiveness.

As we learn about what confession is, we must consider what it is not: Confession is *not* telling everyone we meet of what we have been forgiven.

I once met a woman who had a shocking and tragic history as a stripper and a prostitute before she met Christ. She came to Jesus through a street ministry—Christians witnessing and winning people to Christ where other Christians would not even drive. She longed to be "mainstreamed" into the body of Christ, but felt her history must be told to her local church in order to belong. But they were not ready for her testimony. The ladies in the little country church where she settled were shocked by her story and began to treat her as though she were still carrying the effects of sin and filth. She was viewed with suspicion every time she greeted a man in the church—made worse by the pastor's invitation to "greet one another with a holy hug."

We need wisdom to know with whom we should share our

46

past. If there is still a residue of guilt or temptation, the right people hearing our story can actually help save us from slipping back. The wrong people, however, can actually *send* us back.

Confessing our sins does *not* mean dumping them on an inappropriate person.

I was once speaking at a retreat, and after the first meeting a friend who was attending the retreat approached me: "I have to tell you how much God is doing for me. I used to resent you so much. I was so angry at you that I couldn't even pray or read my Bible. But tonight I gave that all to Jesus and He has taken it all away." Wiping joyful tears away, she turned and left me standing there dumbfounded.

She may have felt freedom, but imagine what I felt. With an entire weekend of ministry still ahead of me, I went to my room wondering what I'd done that could have caused her so much resentment and anger.

Another, wiser friend followed me into my room. "Don't you let that even come near you. That was *her* sin. Not yours."

While that helped, I still hurt.

Confessing that we are sinners is public. Admitting details of sins committed is *not* a public activity, but a private matter between you and the Lord.

"O God, I have been embezzling funds from my employer" is an admission that when made in public becomes public information. "I have been having an affair with my boss" is a confession best made in prayer with a pastor or Christian counselor.

Many lives have been destroyed because the confession of sin was made within the hearing of an unrepentant gossip.

Once we experience the level of trust in our relationship with God that allows us the freedom to confess *anything* to Him, we begin to understand the power of confession.

Confession gives us a time and place to remember a single moment when we know that we brought our sins to Jesus to be covered by His blood. Remembering our confession helps us to have a clean slate with God.

The Israelite soldier at the beginning of this chapter paid for his sins with his life. Jesus paid for our sins with His life. When we confess our sin and accept His payment for us, we accept new possibilities. I like what William James said: "For him who confesses, shams are over and realities have begun."

The realities of forgiveness and God's tender mercies are not available *in case* we sin—but because we do sin.

The great D. L. Moody expressed it this way: "Unless you humble yourself before God in the dust, and confess before Him your iniquities and sins, the gate of heaven, which is open only for sinners saved by grace, must be shut against you forever."

If you were fully convinced of God's merciful forgiveness. is there anything you would want to confess? What?

Think of a time when you shared a confession inappropriately, and write about how you would do that differently after reading this chapter.

Is there some secret sin that you have confessed to God for which you need to pinpoint a time and place of confession? Write it down.

date: _____

date: _____

Some people think that once a sin is confessed it is over, done with, forgiven, and life goes on. That is true, but it's not the whole truth. You can confess the sin and still have the same weakness toward temptation that caused you to sin in the first place. There is much more to learn about dealing with sin after confession. We will learn more about it in the next chapter.

Chapter · 8 ·

The Power of Redemption

"If we confess our sins, he will . . . purify us from all unrighteousness."

1 John 1:9

"DEAR LORD," we pray, "look at what I've done. I've made such a mess of things. Show me how to make it right. I need Your forgiveness, God. I'm sorry."

There is tremendous power available to us when we confess our sins. God's forgiveness is released to us, and we can sense His grace working within us. But, there is more.

David's prayer in Psalm 51 took him deeper than his sin—deeper than the outer action of prayers and confessions. He did not merely pray, "Look at my sin." He said, "Look at *me*." He didn't ask God to make it better, he prayed that he himself might be made pure.

Isn't it easier to admit to a wrong than it is to confess that there is something wrong in us? Aren't we more ready to admit we are guilty of stealing, adultery, careless conversation, over-spending—rather than being a thief, an adulterer, a gossip, an undisciplined person?

So often we resist the "inner look." But the inner look is essential.

While it is not wise to live in continual introspection, it is good to spend time inspecting ourselves occasionally. David's prayer leads him introspectively, but doesn't leave him there: Introspection led him to repentance, which meant permanent change.

We need to take hold of the real nature of repentance.

Repentance is *not* mere confession with an apology tacked on at the end. It is confronting what *I am*, along with what I have done. Only when we are willing to face *what we are* can real cleansing begin.

Here are the steps in God's process:

First, comes guilt—a judgment because of what we have done.

Second, comes shame—the realization of what we are—weak, sick, defective in spirit.

Third, comes conviction—the inner knowing that only God can forgive, only He has the power to help us change.

For the Christian, *conviction* is the positive side of guilt. Sadly, so many of us stay in the guilt and shame of our behaviors simply because we never move beyond confessing our sin and acknowledging our *need*. We may even make a commitment to change, but stop short of receiving the power of God to help us.

Is it any wonder that we get trapped into the cycle of repeating the sin and develop patterns of failure?

The way to freedom is not denying our need, but letting God deal with our heart. Our purpose is not to discover how rotten we are but how righteous He is; not to rehearse our mistakes but to discover His mercy. The result is not more condemnation—but cleansing.

We are fully, even painfully aware of our faults—but we do not focus on our faults. We take courage, and look beyond our faults to our deeper needs. We look to a merciful God, who is able to cleanse us.

———

Ask yourself the following questions:

When you last faced a personal failure or sin, did you pray for

51

forgiveness only, or for cleansing as well?

What area of your life needs changing?

What thoughts has this study brought up in your mind that you don't want to think about?

Pray: Dear Lord, please forgive me for _____, and cleanse me from _____ .

Chapter · 9 ·

The Power of the Past

"*My sin is always before me.*"
Psalm 51:3

LONG AFTER REPENTANCE, long after forgiveness, long
after the relationship with God is fully restored—an uninvited
reminder shakes our peace. Someone you see resembles a person from the past. A song or expression brings the pain of a
buried memory to the surface.

What you believed to be a settled issue feels unsettled once
again. Shame and guilt return, bringing pain.

When old pain comes afresh we feel stuck in the past.
Trapped and frustrated, we may wrongly believe we're paying
the price of past sin even though we confessed it to Christ and
received cleansing. Confused *feelings* of regret and loss cloud
the *reality* of forgiveness and restoration. Is there ever permanent release?

Yes, old memories and painful experiences need not trap
you for the rest of your life. Coming to complete freedom is a
journey that requires many steps taken over a long period of
time.

Openness. When painful memories surface do not hide or
repress them. Hiding them gives them more power—not release.

Honesty. Bring painful memories to God immediately. Remember, the reality is that you did do this thing—but you have also been forgiven for it through confession and repentance. Just as you confessed and asked for cleansing, you can show the memories to God in prayer without reservation.

Give the memory to God. In a very real sense, we disown them. We give up any rights to them and leave them with God by abandoning them to Him. Sometimes it is necessary to go back to the time of confession and remind ourselves of His forgiveness. Occasionally it is good to write down the memory on a piece of paper and then burn it, as a visual reminder of having given the memory to God.

Choose to trust God. God is not going to be reminded of your sin and have second thoughts about forgiving you. Your sin is a settled issue with Him, even though it may not be completely settled within you.

Surrender. Ask God to deal with the part of your heart that has carefully guarded and given room to the memory. Ask Him to cleanse that part of you that has been remembered.

Reclaim lost territory. Take back the right to enjoy whatever has triggered the old memory by making a new memory of restoration and freedom.

Change your mind. Ask God to help you focus on something else.

Praise God. Sing a praise song to the Lord. Recite Bible verses of praise, such as Psalm 145, 149, or 150. I have found it helpful to have these Psalms with me in my purse or briefcase.

Quote passages of Scripture concerning God's love, forgiveness and purpose.

For example: "For I know the plans I have for you," declares the Lord, "plans to prosper you and not to harm you, plans to give you hope and a future. Then you will call upon me and come and pray to me, and I will listen to you. You will seek me and find me when you seek me with all your heart" (Jeremiah 29:11–13).

These steps will help you to walk away from the power of the past—to leave it with God and go your way in peace.

If you were to summarize this process in one prayer, it would go something like this:

Dear God, I give you the memory of _____ . I present it to you in openness and honesty without fear, because I trust in you. I disown this memory. It is now yours because I give it to you. Now, dear Lord, look into my heart. Find that part of me that has been holding on to the past and its memories.

Cleanse me, Lord. And in Jesus' name, I reclaim the joy and sense of restoration that my past failures and painful memories have robbed from me. I can look at (*whatever triggered the memory*), hear this song or _____ without it bringing back feelings of guilt and shame. I am free. I choose now to change my mind and think about you instead. I offer to you my praise.

One verse has meant so much to me for years: "The LORD will fulfill his purpose for me; your love, O LORD, endures forever—do not abandon the works of your hands" (Psalm 138:8). If the Lord would fulfill His purpose for you today, what would He do?

Read Psalm 139:1–4: "O LORD, you have searched me and you know me. You know when I sit and when I rise; you perceive my thoughts from afar. You discern my going out and my lying down; you are familiar with all my ways. Before a word is on my tongue you know it completely, O LORD." How far can you trust Him concerning the private memories you still hold?

According to Jeremiah 29:11, and God's plans to give you "hope and a future," what has the Lord shown you about your future?

1 John 1:9 says: "If we confess our sins, he is faithful and just and will forgive us our sins and purify us from all unrighteousness." How do you know you are walking in sweet fellowship with the Lord?

What are the reasons you can or cannot pray the following: "I'm yours, Lord. The good part, the bad part, the hurt part. All my rationalizing, and all my confusion. All of me—I'm yours. Amen."

Chapter
· 10 ·

Truth,
Not Excuses

"Surely I was sinful at birth, sinful from the time my
mother conceived me."

Psalm 51:5

GIVEN THE SINFUL humanity in which each of us is conceived, it's a wonder any of us ever achieve spiritual freedom.

We are bound by the "human condition," forever stuck. Isn't that right?

No.

We must never forget one all-important factor: While the body may be born into sin, the human spirit was born hungry for God. Our misery is not because we are earthly, but because we have a potential for the heavenly.

I have yet to hear anyone say, "I came from a totally healthy, functional family. My parents were fully prepared to be parents, professional and fair, without flaw in their skills to bring up children. I got everything from them I needed." Even at its best, humanity lacks.

While we can't choose the parents to whom we are born, the circumstances of conception, or the condition of our early days, now that we are adults we *can* choose what we will become. The greater the task of overcoming our beginning, the greater the opportunity to experience God's mercy and healing. And the greater our chance for accomplishment and personal reward.

Our hope is not dependent upon our beginning, but upon our future.

List three things from your childhood that you have overcome:

1. _____
2. _____
3. _____

List the names of three overcomers you know or know about:

1. _____
2. _____
3. _____

If you could overcome your childhood—your beginning—how would your life change?

In many ways, we overcome the memories of the sin that has been done *to* us in the same way we overcome the memories of sin done *by* us. (Review chapter nine.) But with one major addition: We are the ones who must release forgiveness.

Many people I know are dealing with childhood hurts and long-term family issues, and they are learning to forgive. That is good, and it's right. And while it's important, it is not the matter I am referring to here. I am addressing the temptation to *use our past experiences to excuse present behaviors.* Past experiences help us to understand our present behavior, but not to excuse it.

David says in his prayer that his problems are long-standing—based on the human condition, born *in* him as in all of us. We are, unfortunately, fully human.

The temptation is to use our humanity as an excuse to fall back into our old ways. And so we set ourselves up to fall to the same old temptations, commit the same old cycle over and over.

The way forward is through *surrender.*

You may protest that you've dealt with sinful issues through confession and repentance. You've learned to release memories and deal with your painful past. Isn't that enough?

No. We must also surrender our past, our present, and our

58

future. We must surrender ourselves—our very hearts.

What is it that always gets in the way of our surrender? Could it be fear—fear that we won't get something we want, or won't be able to do something we want to do? Fear that if we are surrendered we will be weak and won't be respected or treated with love?

If we do not surrender, we doom ourselves to be stuck in an unending struggle with sin and self.

Surrender, in godly terms, means to set our sights on building that perfect-love relationship with One who loves us perfectly. It is a growing thing, which will challenge us every day.

Surrender is the only way to experience for ourselves— deep within, in our heart of hearts—God's grace.

Surrender is the greatest prerequisite for a new heart. Let the reality of the human condition into which you were born bring you to this point of surrender.

Do you need a new heart?

What areas are you still reluctant to surrender?

Can God be trusted with your unsurrendered areas?

Can *you* trust Him? Why—or why not?

If you still have trouble surrendering, bring that with you. Surrender even that inability to Him. You are on the threshold of a wonderful new depth of relationship with God. This is not the time to go back, but to go on. A whole new dimension of your life with our perfect Savior, Jesus Christ, is waiting to be explored.

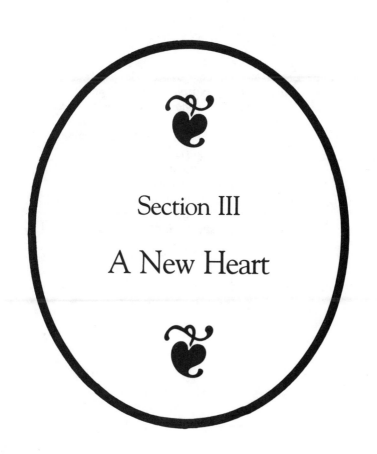

Section III

A New Heart

Surely you desire truth in the inner parts;
    you teach me wisdom in the inmost place.
Cleanse me with hyssop, and I will be clean;
    wash me, and I will be whiter than snow.
Let me hear joy and gladness;
    let the bones you have crushed rejoice.
Hide your face from my sins
    and blot out all my iniquity.
Create in me a pure heart, O God,
    renew a steadfast spirit within me.

PSALM 51:6

"TO BE PERFECTLY HONEST. . . ."

"To tell you the truth. . . ."

Many of us use these cliches, and make it sound as if we are about to disclose an intimate secret, when in fact we are only about to share an opinion. But we speak in this way to convince others that it's a privilege to hear what we're about to tell them.

We have many ways to sound like we are open and transparent, when we are really safely hiding our tender selves.

It is not always wrong to hold matters and feelings in private. It can be devastating to share your innermost secrets with an untrustworthy person. But hiding from God is not healthy. We must admit to ourselves and to God two things. One, that we have a soul. And two, what condition it is in.

In past chapters, we have seen that David has called upon the mercy of God, confronted his sin and himself, and that he is deeply repentant. In this section we will follow him as he admits that need goes even deeper. His actions have been examined and his sin forgiven—now he is ready to address the condition of his soul.

Chapter · 11 ·

The Old Heart

"Surely you desire truth in the inner parts; you teach me wisdom in the inmost place."

Psalm 51:6

"I HAVE HANDED JESUS the key to my secret hideout," says Paddy Baker. Paddy has learned the principle of truth in the inner part—wisdom in the inmost place.

Is your secret hideout locked against God? Are you willing to hand Jesus the key?

The inward part is the *I am* part—not the *I do* part. Just like David, we also have an *I am* part—it's most likely a secret hideout. But many of us do not want to address it.

The *I am* can be filled with lies and shame. Sometimes lies and shame have been put there by others—parents, siblings, church, friends. Other times we have filled our secret hideouts with lies about ourselves and shame about our past.

In either case, our soul may feel so much pain, that to survive we have chosen to avoid the *I am* part of ourselves. We learn to focus on what we *do* as a basis for our worth. To replace lies and shame with truth in the inward part, we will need to face the lies and confront the shame.

Often, this will mean facing sin and anger, confronting

resentments, experiencing disappointments, or feeling the pain of abuse or abandonment. Those emotions are not who we *are*, they are only the defenses we have set up to protect our inward part. But these defenses can become so strong that sometimes even *we* cannot get in behind them.

To get in touch with the inward part, we must stop treating ourselves like the enemy. We must give ourselves permission to go in—not to make the private sector of our being accessible to everyone, but certainly opening up to *ourselves* and to Jesus Christ, our loving Savior.

When we discover the truth inwardly, we will also discover the strength to face the lies we have believed about ourselves—the falsehoods on which we have based our poor sense of worth.

Only when we persevere and break through barricades of defensive emotions will we find peace, worth, and hope that comes from a new sense of value. Our new value is based on *who we are*, not on what we have done or failed to do.

To many, exploring the inward part is a scary idea. Walking back into pain and disappointment is too overwhelming. That's why David's prayer is so helpful. David invited God to be there with him: "You teach me wisdom in the inmost place."

How do we let God into the inward part? Let me illustrate:

In my house I have a special room. Inside that special room I keep a cedar chest, and in it is a box that holds a notebook with a very private collection—my thoughts, fears, and prayers written during a particularly difficult period in my life. In the chest I also keep a few other treasures: a couple of tiny sweaters, booties, and bonnets worn by my babies, along with snippets of baby hair. This chest in the special room in my house may be compared to my secret heart and what I keep in it.

Inside my self, within my heart, is my *secret heart*, a kind of emotional cedar chest. In that place I keep spiritual souvenirs—memories, hopes, secret prayers, and dreams. I don't let anyone in that private place, just as I do not let anyone rummage around in my cedar chest. No one can really understand or appreciate the value of the little treasures I keep there.

Inside my treasure box in my cedar chest there are many things that have precious meaning only to me: cards made so carefully by the little hands of my children, the postcard I sent my grandpa when I was eight, the napkin with music notes written on it by my daughter Rhonda when she was only five.

I have treasures within my heart of hearts as well. I may have forgotten that some of them are there, but they are there just the same. If I am to learn wisdom—God's wisdom—in my secret heart, it will be necessary to let Him see what I keep there. He will not push His way in. I must voluntarily unlock my heart of hearts, take out my treasures, and show them to Him, one by one. I must be willing to let Him hold each emotional souvenir I keep there—my cherished personal thoughts, my secret hopes, my precious memories, my private pain, and secret sufferings—each and every one.

Then, I need to ask Him what to do with each one. Do I need to clean out some things to make room for healthier attitudes and future memories? If I find such courage, it will be because I have been willing to become vulnerable enough to let God see what I have been keeping there. I must become willing to let God replace with His promises all the painful broken ones I have been saving, tied up and neatly bundled with ribbons of disappointment—to receive new dreams for my broken ones, to receive the promise of new potential in trade for all my failures.

Only God can replace pain with wholeness, unforgiveness with forgiveness, disappointment with hope. He alone has the ability to replace fantasy with reality, to trade my sadness for joy.

A strange thing happens when we let God teach us wisdom in the secret heart—we find some things we could not bear to throw out before turn into musty rags we can no longer bear to keep.

Ask yourself: How do I protect my inward self?

Remember a time when you mistakenly trusted someone with a part of yourself and they hurt you with what you shared. Forgive that person and write out that forgiveness.

Which emotion are you most afraid of confronting when you explore your inward part?

How does that emotion protect you?

Can you trust God to protect you, instead of allowing that emotion to guard you? How do you know?

If you knew you were going to let God see what you keep in your secret heart, what would you like to remove beforehand?

Remembering that God will not rummage through your secret heart, but that you must show Him each item there, what do you want to show Him first?

What do you want to keep for another time? He is patient; He will wait until you are ready.

Chapter · 12 ·

More Than Motions

"Cleanse me with hyssop, and I will be clean; wash me, and I will be whiter than snow."

Psalm 51:7

THE RITUALS OF RELIGION can never satisfactorily replace a living relationship with God. Even though David had a deep appreciation for rituals, he had a grasp on the relational dimension that not many had in his day. He was well-versed in the ceremonial side of his religion—but he cultivated the relational side even more. The ritualistic part gave him opportunity to act out his confession and abandonment of sin, but did nothing to *change* him. Character change, and the accompanying personal freedom, only comes from heart change. And that comes only through a thorough cleansing.

We have our own rituals of religion. We may say that we don't when in fact we do. It may not be in the structure or form of a public worship service, but in the more personal rituals that allow us to act out our confession and abandonment of sin, but do nothing to change us.

For example, how many of us pray to God to get to the "heart of the matter," solve the problem, give us an answer, or change a situation? We pray, "God, I want to talk to you about my husband," or "Lord, I want to talk to you about my lousy attitude." But how many of us say, "Lord God, please talk to me about my marriage," or "Dear Father, please speak to me about my lousy attitude."

So many times we have sought God for forgiveness, and avoided His gentle invitation for cleansing. We confess our sins, but stop short of washing our hearts. We want the record cleared, but do we want a clean heart?

When we resist change on the inside, we set ourselves up for repeated failure. I have discovered that if I only confess the sin—even truly and totally repent—but do not let God in to clean house in my secret heart, then I find a way to hang on to vulnerabilities that cause me to trip over the same temptation again. By not letting God do a thorough work of cleansing in me, I make it easier to sin again.

It is in this light that I have asked myself these questions:

1. Do I really want to be cleansed, or do I only want to be forgiven?
2. Do I want to be changed, or only excused?
3. When I cry out to God concerning a sin, am I asking for understanding and tolerance, or do I want purity?

Think of a sin from which you have recently repented. You may or may not want to write it down.

Ask yourself the three questions above and consider your response. Add your own comments.

If you were to go back and pray the prayer of Psalm 51:7 what would you change? Your answers and mine determine whether or not we have a relationship with God or simply a religion.

What do you have?

Which do you prefer?

Chapter · 13 ·

Rejoicing!

"Let me hear joy and gladness; let the bones you have crushed rejoice."

Psalm 51:8

YOU HAVE FAILED.

You've done something wrong—and what is worse, you knew it was wrong at the time but did it anyway.

Maybe it's not something you have done. Maybe it's an attitude you've been nurturing, or impure thoughts you've been entertaining. In any case you are sensing the guilt. Even though you haven't acted on your thoughts you still feel impure and unable to come to God.

This is not what God has for you. Your relationship with Him was closer and better in previous days. The knot in your stomach hardly ever goes away. You may try to justify it by pointing out your needs, your hurts, your loneliness, your past. But the justification is beginning to sound shallow, even to you. It's been a long time since you heard the sounds of joy and gladness coming from within. Your whole life is suffering; your joy is lacking because of this awful *thing* in your life.

Church attendance is a drudge. Should the speaker give a challenge or an invitation to come forward for prayer you would find it necessary to either leave the service or hang tightly on to the pew in front of you to keep from responding.

This is what many people experience when they come face-to-face with conviction. Conviction is that sense of knowing what you know about yourself and your sin (which no one else knows) along with the panic of knowing God knows!

Many have experienced physical symptoms when under conviction—pounding heart, sweaty palms, even stomach cramps. The more we resist, the more intense the symptoms become.

Once we can admit that we are "under conviction" and take the very first step toward loving God who has shown us our sin, we experience a rush of hope. The charade is finished, the mask can come off, and we can be real again. Correction is here, forgiveness is available, and restoration can begin.

Confession and repentance is the only way to respond to the conviction of God's Holy Spirit. Once this happens, change begins. Attitudes can be challenged and changed. Lies can be exposed to the truth. Cover-ups become a thing of the past and freedom is the promise of the future. Truth invades the repentant human spirit in a way that corrects and encourages at the same time.

God is not going to hurt you when you repent. He will not expose all your shortcomings and failures to those around you. He is not going to stand you in the front of the congregation and hurl accusations and insults at you. He wants to forgive, to heal, and to help us go on with our lives. He wants to help us live in ways that are both pleasing to Him and hopeful to us.

Once conviction and correction have done their work, we can enter a total and complete process of recovery. The effects of sin can be washed away. Some people experience immediate release and supernatural recovery. Others enter a longer time of restoration. Strength for restitution is given along with the power to live a disciplined life.

Sometimes the work that follows our surrender to God takes time and effort. But after repentance comes restoration—in our relationships, our families, our personalities, and our self-worth.

Too often we act as though we are a people whose sins are

only found out, not forgiven. We face the sin, confess it, and repent. But then instead of leaving the guilt, we insist on carrying it. Why? If a sin is forgiven, there is no more guilt!

Like David, we can ask for God to let us once again feel the joy and gladness that comes from a clean heart.

When did the Holy Spirit last convict you—spotlight some area of your life that needed changing?

What is the difference between conviction and condemnation?

What did you feel?

Did you repent?

What is there to prevent you from experiencing joy? Rejoice, Christian—*rejoice!*

Chapter
· 14 ·

Hope

"Hide your face from my sin and blot out all my iniquity."

Psalm 51:9

WHAT A WONDERFUL THOUGHT—that there is actually a way to get rid of all the iniquity that seems to stubbornly reside within. What a joy to know that our prayer life can truly go beyond prayers like:

"You are so pure, my God, and I am so full of sin. Dear Lord, can't You find a way to see beyond a sinful broken past—to see me?"

There is a way. It is possible for the barriers that come between us and God to be broken.

God knows we want to be free. He knows we don't always choose the barriers between us. He wants us to be free, too.

And because He desires to be close to us, He sent Jesus. Jesus doesn't go around the sin barrier. He doesn't go over it, or merely poke a hole in it. *He removes it.*

You can't remove sin and neither can I. But we can co-operate with Jesus as He does—and in fact, He can't do it without us. He uses our surrender to break down what is between us.

In the past we have surrendered to our sins, yielded to the guilt. But no longer. Now we choose to surrender only to Him.

We no longer fear that God sees only sin: He sees us! And what's more, He likes what He sees.

The sin issue is finally resolved, taken to the cross with Jesus and nailed there. It is finished.

———

Do you believe the issue is settled?

Do you act as if you believe it?

Knowing what you now know about God and His deep love and compassion for you, is there anything left in your life that you still do not want God to see? What is it?

When He looks at you, what do you want Him to see?

Is there anything in your life that is a barrier to His seeing you as you are?

Chapter · 15 ·

A New Heart

"Create in me a pure heart, O God, and renew a steadfast spirit within me."

Psalm 51:10

ARE YOU TIRED OF MAKING commitments to change, only to fail within the first twenty-four hours? What if there were a way for you to begin making firm commitments and *keeping* them?

Isn't it time for a radical departure from defeat, and the destruction it leaves behind?

That would take a whole new approach, wouldn't it? A new heart. Not a redecorated or a redesigned heart. Not made out of the old one—a *new* heart.

That's what David's prayer was all about. He wasn't asking God for change—he asked God to create within him something totally new.

Create means to make something out of nothing. David knew his need, and he knew his God. Only God could answer this prayer. Think of it. David could have approached his sin quite differently. For example, I have been told there was a time when the hand of a thief was cut off. What if David had approached the sin in his life with such a simplistic and drastic solution? Would he have ordered his eye gouged out, since he had first *looked* at Bathsheba with lust?

David's prayer for a new heart reveals his understanding; his physical body was not the root of his sin, his heart was. Just as cutting off a hand cannot remove stealing from one's heart, gouging out an eye does not change a lusting heart. Stealing and lusting can only be changed by an inner work. Consistency and integrity are found in a steadfast spirit—and this is a work only God can do.

A new heart means new desires and willingness to let go of old ones; it means freedom from guilt and a willingness to let go of old guilt; it means new direction and letting go of old patterns; it means new motives, new purpose, and new attitudes. It means a brand-new me.

A new heart comes with a high price, and that price is to give up the old me. Are you willing to pay the price?

Do you want to leave behind unhealthy relationships? Are you tired of rehearsing the past and planning your future by your mistakes? Are you paying for your past with present potential, contentment, and peace? We embrace unhealthy habits. Drugs, alcohol, and promiscuity are obviously destructive—but also damaging are overspending, overeating, over-committing, worry, anger, and unforgiveness. And the price we pay is self-control, wholeness, and individual worth.

We also worship false gods, such as money, recognition, physical appearance, and perfectionism. We lose our tolerance of anything less than financial prosperity, popularity, and power. And we pay the price of losing our compassion toward those who suffer or are poor. We exchange contentment for strife and surrender our true identity.

All inner change requires is a simple prayer: "Lord, please change me. Where there has been destruction, renew me; where sickness, heal me. Instead of false worship, I choose a relationship with You. I'm not asking for a dramatic change in my life, but in me."

What are some of the things in you or your life that you have been trying to change without God's help?

If you were given a new heart, what are some things from your old heart that would have to be sacrificed?

If God were to renew a steadfast spirit within you, what things in your life would change?

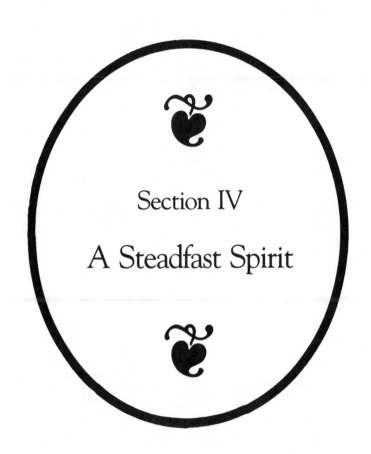

Section IV

A Steadfast Spirit

But now this is what the LORD says—
He who created you, O Jacob,
He who formed you, O Israel:
"Fear not, for I have redeemed you;
  I have summoned you by name; you are mine."

ISAIAH 43:1

I LIVE IN EARTHQUAKE COUNTRY. California has a long history of shaky ground and hidden faults that can change thousands of lives within seconds.

Structures a century old and thought to be solid and secure can walk off their foundations and collapse when the earth beneath them moves. Public awareness campaigns and disaster drills can never prepare you for the sudden terror that strikes when the room starts rocking while the once-solid earth below rolls and shakes. Sidewalks rise then suddenly drop beneath pedestrians, causing feelings of nausea and imbalance. Anxiety and panic spreads following the first jolt, knowing that within the next 48 hours aftershocks can continue the destruction.

A strong earthquake can cause as much devastation as a tornado. Unfortunately, not all of the damage appears immediately. Minor cracks can develop and reveal major structural damage days and weeks later.

Yes, we in California live on shaky ground. We know it, and we live with the uncertainty of it every day. We make our emergency plans for contacting family members, pack away food, water supplies, and first-aid kits; and we send blankets to the school supply closet in case "the big one" hits. And then we go about our business as usual.

Many of us live on shaky ground spiritually. We have been rocked, dropped, and shaken by some event that left us damaged and uncertain of our footing.

We have waited for the aftershocks, and hoped to survive further hurts and devastation. It's time to find a new foundation on secure and solid ground.

Steadfastness: what a wonderful, solid word. Your spiritual life can be built to "earthquake standards"—that is, on biblical principles. Yes, times of shaking will come, but your life will be built to withstand even the most devastating quake.

Steadfastness is built on knowing and believing these five principles:

1. God says I am accepted—that I belong to Him—in the Beloved.
2. God says I am no longer unclean—but clean clear through.
3. God says I am free from judgment, and that I am free indeed.
4. God says He looks on me with joy—that He likes me.
5. God says I may throw off my mourning and rejoice— it's time to celebrate!

Chapter · 16 ·

Strangers in the Land

"Fear not, for I have redeemed you; I have summoned you by name; you are mine."

Isaiah 43:1

"I DON'T FIT HERE," Barbara said. "Usually I know every woman at a retreat. But this time I feel so alone."

"I can't find my place," Janet confided that same day. "I never guessed how difficult it would be to move to a new town and change churches."

"There's no place for me here," Patty cried. "I'm so used to being involved. I've been here six months, and I'm still out of it."

Being the new person in a group often brings feelings of alienation. Starting over, being on the outside, and not understanding the history of the new place is uncomfortable. Hearing inside jokes and not catching the meaning makes it worse.

Being an outsider doesn't just happen when you change locations physically, it also happens when you come through a time of tremendous growth or change. There are times when even the familiar looks different because of a new perspective.

Moses fled the Egyptians. Raised as one of them, he became an outsider after he killed one of them. All his life he had lived as one of them. Now he was alienated. Not only his perspective, but his whole life changed after the experience with the burning bush (Exodus 3). Being an outsider wasn't a pleasant experience for Moses.

Others in the Bible knew what it was to be an outsider.

Living on the run and hiding wasn't fun for David. Paul certainly knew what it was to live as a loner. But all of them—Moses, David, and Paul also knew what it was to belong to God.

Belonging to God and being committed to His purpose means living "separated" lives. Singled out for service often means being able to stand alone without feeling abandoned. Many leaders report feeling cut off from the crowd.

After the creation of your new heart, before the beginning of your new start, God wants to renew a steadfast spirit within you. That spirit comes only when you are willing to depend upon God and Him alone for your sense of belonging. He has called you by name. You are His.

There are advantages to this separateness. Objectivity, quietness, safety, and true identity are based on our willingness to be alone with God as a part of our routine. Being His beloved is more important than being a part of the inner circle at church. Belonging to Him alone is more of a priority than belonging to the inside social track.

Our busy lives, our need for friends and social affirmation, often prevent us from being in that quiet separate place. We let ourselves get over-involved with people, but neglect our need to be alone with God. While surrounding ourselves with friends, we can deny the realization that we are really longing for God.

Even when we see our need to reserve a part of our life and time for God, He seems so far away. How can we make time for aloneness with Him without succumbing to our fear of being alone with Him? How can we bridge the gap between our need for God and our need for people? Between our need for quietness and our need for noise? Between our need for solitude and our need for recognition?

How can we ever reach Him without our emotional needs sabotaging our desire to be closer to Him?

Look at Jesus' parable in Luke 15: A wayward son is returning home. We can only imagine the things he said to himself on his way. What would he say to his father? Should he knock or go right through the door? Should he come up the front walk or down the alley to the servants' door?

None of his planned speeches would be heard. He didn't have to decide whether to use the front or the back door. His father was waiting to meet his son on the road:

"But while he was still a long way off, his father saw him and was filled with compassion for him; he ran to his son, threw his arms around him and kissed him" (Luke 15:20).

Father-God is waiting for you. He wants to give you a sense of belonging that no person, no group, no church, no job, no position can ever give you. He wants to tell you how much He loves you. He wants to show you how you fit into His family. He wants you to feel comfortable in your belonging to Him. Feeling alienated while you live in this life only means that you and I are not yet home.

You may never feel a part of the "in crowd" again. But it doesn't matter, you belong to God and are accepted in the Beloved. You have the steadfastness that comes from knowing you are God's.

———————

Write your first name: ——————————————
If God would speak your name, how would it sound to you?

For the next five minutes, sit in quietness. No radio, no tape, no praise music. Close your Bible and hold it close to you. Acknowledge that God has spoken to you and that every promise in your Bible is yours. Every revelation of Christ from Genesis through Revelation is for you. Simply let the realization of your living, loving Savior penetrate into your spirit.

You belong to God. You are accepted by Him. You have meaning; you have purpose. He has called you by name, and you are His. What difference does this knowledge make to you?

What difference does it make *in* you?

Chapter · 17 ·

Clean Clear Through

"The clothing, or the woven or knitted material, or any leather article that has been washed and is rid of the mildew, must be washed again, and it will be clean."

Leviticus 13:58

MY GRANDMA SAMPSON used to set up her washing machine and two rinse tubs right in her kitchen. She would sort the clothes into piles. Whites first, then towels, followed by colored clothes, and finally workclothes.

She would treat spots according to the fabric as well as what made the spot. Grandpa's workpants were often stained with black grease, and so Grandma rubbed them with lard. Whites were given a stiff dose of Purex bleach, which made the whole house smell sterile.

In the second rinse tub she put a small dark waxy block she called *bluing*. "It makes things extra nice," she explained. And it also made the kitchen smell sweeter after the bleach.

I loved laundry day at Grandma's. Everything that looked and smelled dirty in the morning was clean, bright, and folded neatly by evening. Towels were ready to be used again. Aprons and shirts were washed and starched and sprinkled, wrapped in a large tablecloth and a thick towel, ready for ironing the next day. Sheets were folded neatly and placed on the shelf, making the whole closet smell fresh.

Grandma was an expert at laundry. There was no soiled spot Grandma didn't tackle and only a few she couldn't erase. It was a miracle.

Repentance is the laundry day of the spirit. It is a time of sorting, deep cleaning, followed by rest and preparation to be used again.

What a wonder it is to be clean again—knowing there is no spot God cannot totally eradicate! It is a miracle almost too marvelous to understand.

Many remember where the spot was. I do sometimes, and you probably do, too. But when God does a cleansing, He does it thoroughly. It does no good to remember where the dirt was. Many want to wear a badge over the cleansed area as a reminder. Some mark the spot and call it a testimony.

When God does a work, let it be complete. The testimony is not about the horrendous thing you did that needed cleansing, it is about the miraculous work Jesus did!

"God made him who had no sin to be sin for us, so that in him we might become the righteousness of God" (2 Corinthians 5:21).

We are clean. Not in ourselves, but because of Jesus.

If God cleansed us the way *we* think He should, our whole lives would be burned and reeking with the smell of bleach. But God didn't send bleach to fade the spot, He spilled the precious blood of His Son, Jesus, to remove it completely.

The fragrance of a life cleansed by Jesus' blood is so much fresher than any of Grandma's sheets rinsed in bluing and hung in the warm sunshine to dry. A cleansed life gives off the aroma of service and sacrifice. The incense of joy. The perfume of commitment. The sweetness of contentment and satisfaction.

This is the life of the born-again believer—the unclean sinner made clean by an act of God. This is also the story of the tired, battered Christian renewed by God's mercy, sustained by His grace. This is a picture of a "blessed one" empowered to live in peace, renewed in spirit to live a steadfast life.

You and I are clean—clean clear through.

"Blessed are those who wash their robes, that they may have the right to the tree of life and may go through the gates into the city" (Revelation 22:14).

———————

If you were part of God's laundry, where would He put you where you would be ready for service?

With the towels and washcloths. (Ready to be used to wipe the tears and sweat of tired and hurting people.)

With the clean sheets. (Providing a fresh place of comfort for those who are weary.)

With the aprons, tablecloths, and potholders. (Ready to be used as He prepares food for hungry souls.)

With the workclothes. (Ready to go into His field and help with the harvest.)

If you really believed that God has made you clean—clean clear through, how would that change your life?

How would it change the way you look at your past?

How would it change the way you look at your future?

What would you like to say to God about being clean?

What words of praise for the blood of Jesus express how you feel about being clean again?

Chapter
· 18 ·

Free Indeed!

"If the Son sets you free, you will be free indeed."
John 8:36

IMAGINE BEING ARRESTED, hauled off to jail, finally taken to court. Every charge against you is true, every shred of evidence solid. Think how you would feel knowing you will be found guilty and that the punishment for your crime is death.

This is where we all stand before accepting Jesus. Sin put us under the judgment of God. But that was before we accepted Jesus. Knowing Him as our Savior makes an amazing difference.

Imagine the same courtroom scene again. This time it is near the end of the trial. The guilty verdict has been handed down and the sentence has been read—death.

The judge asks, "Do you have anything to say in your behalf?"

"I do not," you reply. "I am guilty as charged."

"Your honor!" A strong voice rings out.

The courtroom falls under a great hush as a gentle, yet powerful figure rises and moves forward.

"May I approach the bench on behalf of the defendant?"

The request is granted.

Walking forward to face the judge, Jesus speaks. "I have already paid the price for these sins. I have come to set this one free."

"You accept this sinful person's debt?"

Turning toward you—face-to-face, His eyes burning into your spirit—He speaks ever so gently. His tender voice is clear and deep with emotion.

"If the defendant will accept my payment," says the Beloved One. And then He opens His hands to reveal deep scars just above the wrists.

Then Jesus faces the judge, displaying the scars for everyone in the courtroom to see.

The judge's eyes fill with tears as he looks from the scars to search your face for an answer.

"Do you accept this man's payment?" he asks.

It's up to you. You have the final say. Jesus is ready to take the sentence in your place. It is a sentence He has already fulfilled. It is yours; it is your freedom, if you will accept Him.

His payment does not take away the fact that you have sinned, but it will save you from the punishment. It will not give you back wasted years, but it will give you a free future.

Once you accept His death as payment for your sin, nothing you have ever done will ever be charged to your account again.

No, you can't change the past, but you can be free from it. You may not be able to erase hurtful memories and regret, but you can be free of the guilt.

You can be free to live a holy life. Free to live a surrendered life. God says that when you accept Jesus Christ as your Savior, *you are free.*

"God made him who had no sin to be sin for us, so that in him we might become the righteousness of God" (2 Corinthians 5:21).

You have nothing to fear, nothing to hide, no shame to bear. There is no bondage too strong for God's love to shatter. You are a new creation. The old is gone, the new is come. God declares you free.

Will you accept freedom?

Will you embrace the belief that you are free from His judgment?

List several ways in which you still accept guilt and shame instead of Christ's freedom.

If you really believed that you were completely free from judgment how would that change the way you look at your past?

How would it change the way you relate to people?

How would it change the way you look at your future?

I Am
Liked

*"The LORD your God is with you, he is mighty to save.
He will take great delight in you, he will quiet you with
his love, he will rejoice over you with singing."*

Zephaniah 3:17

GOD LIKES ME. What a daring thought!

We know God loves us. He has to. We are part of the
world and He *loves* the whole world. Having accepted Jesus as
Savior secures God's love for us.

But to think that God not only loves—but likes us!

Recently something brought this little migrant thought
back to me:

I watched my baby play in the park. That's all I did. Just
watched her play. I watched her climb on the jungle gym,
slide down the small slide, and finally venture over to the
bigger spiral slide. She climbed the ladder, sat down, and slid
round and round until her little feet plopped safely in the sand
below. Then she wandered over to the swing and played there
a while.

All the time, I watched from the shady gazebo several feet
away.

Eventually, she approached the merry-go-round. Soon she

was pushing it around and around to the glee of the other children.

My baby is twenty-six years old, and she was entertaining her own babies that day. And I watched her, and loved watching. I love her.

I like how she carefully hovers over her little ones, yet gives them room to experiment and explore. I like how she ties their loose shoestrings, pats their little bottoms, and runs her long slender fingers through their hair.

She clearly enjoys her children. She plays with them—as much for her enjoyment as for theirs.

She likes them, I thought. *And I like her.*

And I like you, the Father seemed to whisper into my spirit. Bright, wonderful, and warm was the thought.

That day I caught a glimpse of a loving Father, watching over me as I have watched over my own children. I see Him now, delighted when He sees that what He has put into us is passed on to others. He likes us when He sees us at play, secure and happy in Him.

Paul says it this way:

"For he chose us in him before the creation of the world to be holy and blameless in his sight. In love he predestined us to be adopted as his sons through Jesus Christ, in accordance with his pleasure and will—to the praise of his glorious grace, which he has freely given us in the One he loves" (Ephesians 1:4–6).

Yes, God looks on us with joy. An essential part of living in steadfastness is to know that God not only loves us, but likes us.

When we are secure in the *like* of God as much as in His love, verses like 2 Chronicles 16:9 take on an entire new depth and meaning:

"For the eyes of the LORD range throughout the earth to strengthen those whose hearts are fully committed to him."

See yourself face-to-face with your heavenly Father. Now look into His eyes—see the tenderness there. See the love there. See joy there.

Is thinking that God *likes* you an easy or difficult concept? Explain.

Think of someone you really like. _____

List the reasons why you like that person.

Find an opportunity to tell someone, "You know, I really *like* you." That is a powerful statement.

Chapter · 20 ·

Let's Celebrate

"There is a time for everything, and a season for every activity under heaven . . . a time to weep and a time to laugh, a time to mourn and a time to dance."

Ecclesiastes 3:1, 4

WE MAY PLAN OUR ACTIVITIES around the months and days on the calendar, but we mark our lives and organize our memories around events.

"Before Johnny was born. . . ."

"After Sarah came. . . ."

"After the war. . . ."

"Before the accident. . . ."

"After I lost my job. . . ."

Whatever prompted you to buy this book may very well be one of those significant events in your life. You probably somehow "connected" the promise of the title, *A New Heart— A New Start*, to your need to somehow find a fresh beginning. To find the strength to go on. To leave the way things *were* in order to find the way you hope they *can be*.

Today is the day you can make a choice between living in the pain of the past or letting all you've learned produce wisdom, compassion, depth, and even joy within you.

"You have sown in tears, it is time to lift your weary head, wipe your teary eyes and begin to sing songs of rejoicing" (Psalm 126:5–6).

Let this day be a significant one. Let this day be an event, a milestone you can point to and say, "That was the day I chose joy! That was the day I let the Lord of my life turn my sorrow into singing—my mourning into celebration." (See Esther 9:22.)

"That was the day I stood from the ashes of regret and accepted a crown of beauty on my head. The day I submitted to God and let Him anoint my head with the oil of gladness— the day I stopped mourning over my failures and accepted the hope of a new start. It was the day I took off the robes of despair and put on a garment of praise." (See Isaiah 61:3.)

Just as surely as God called us to repentance, He calls us now to joy.

Just as certain painful events can cause our lives to come to a full stop, God calls us now to a new start.

Just as pain and sorrow brought us to tears of remorse and regret, God calls us now to celebrate.

It's the appropriate time—the *appointed* time—to look within once again. This time, find that little spark of joy flickering there. Blowing ever so gently upon it, see it glow brighter and brighter then explode into laughing flames of celebration.

It's okay to feel good again. To laugh and sing again. God says we may throw off our mourning and rejoice!

It's time to plan a celebration. To make life fun again. It will take as much determination and commitment to celebrate as it ever did to repent and surrender. Why not try some of these suggestions:

1. Tonight, even if you are all alone, set your table with the best dishes you have. If anyone asks, tell them it is just for fun.
2. Put a fresh flower in a bud vase, with a note of encouragement or scripture in a place you will find it first thing tomorrow morning.
3. Write out a favorite verse of promise and put it on your car visor or dash.

4. Make plans to see a friend this weekend.
5. Take a long walk in a natural setting or park.
6. Plan what you will wear to church a few days in advance and add some special touches to it—different earrings, new stockings, a different scarf or shoes.
7. Wear perfume to bed—just for yourself.
8. Indulge in a bubble bath and use *two* towels.
9. Paint your toenails a bright, pretty color.
10. Clean and reorganize a closet in a spirit of celebration and excitement.
11. Change something in your living room—rehang your pictures, rearrange the furniture, clean the curtains or drapes.
12. Read a magazine, browse a catalog, or read a novel.
13. Try a new vegetable.
14. Change the sheets on your bed in the middle of the week.
15. Drink a cup of gourmet coffee in a china cup. (Sitting up in bed, on clean sheets, wearing perfume while reading the magazine would be wonderful.)

———————

How will you celebrate today?

How could you celebrate and rejoice this next weekend?

n were to become a part of you, how would your

If you were to say some new, celebrative, rejoicing words of praise to God, what would they be?

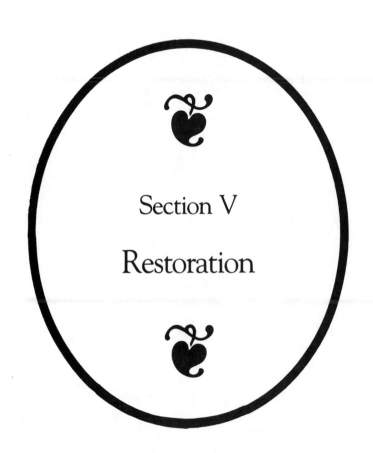

Section V

Restoration

*D*o not cast me from your presence
  or take your Holy Spirit from me.
Restore to me the joy of your salvation
  and grant me a willing spirit, to sustain me.

PSALM 51:11–12

BELIEVE IT OR NOT, nothing can separate us from God's love. Let Paul's promise awaken your spirit with that truth:

"For I am convinced that neither death nor life, neither angels nor demons, neither the present nor the future, nor any powers, neither height nor depth, nor anything else in all creation, will be able to separate us from the love of God that is in Christ Jesus our Lord" (Romans 8:38–39).

Most Christians I know have experienced periods of spiritual dryness. Times when there is a lack of confidence and felt power in our lives can be the result of something that causes static in our relationship with God—something perhaps hidden deep within our hearts.

As Isaiah said, "Your iniquities have separated you from your God; your sins have hidden his face from you, so that he will not hear" (59:2).

If that is your experience, then today more than ever you need the process of Psalm 51—with its promise of restoration.

Most of us want an instant answer—and wouldn't that be nice? But in reality, restoration takes longer than a miracle; but is no less miraculous. It is the deep healing of the soul, by means of turning one back to God in restored fellowship and intimacy. The process of restoration takes time well-spent in reflection, repentance, and return to God's Word and His ways.

David is asking for restoration when he says, "Don't leave me, God. Let me sense your presence." Can you detect a different tone? No longer arrogant, but repentant, his prayer reveals his felt need for God's anointing and presence.

David never read Psalm 51. He lived it. In doing so he led the way on the path to healing and restoration. What he prayed by faith alone, we can pray according to God's promise. What God did for David He will do for you and me.

David is defenseless in his prayer: "Without you, I can *do* nothing." Hear his helplessness: "Without you, I *am* nothing."

Can you identify with David? In the same way he prayed, can you admit your utter defenselessness? Are you aware that without Him *you* can do nothing? (See John 15:6.)

God has always promised restoration to those who return to Him:

"I am with you and will watch over you wherever you go, and I will bring you back to this land. I will not leave you until I have done what I have promised you" (Genesis 28:15).

Look also to the writings of Isaiah. David did not have the advantage we have of seeing the book of Isaiah, or of hearing how God desired to restore Israel. While he could only look forward to the *hope* of a Messiah—you and I can look to the *reality* of our Savior. What David did by raw faith, we can do by relying on the promises of God's Word.

Let the words of Isaiah encourage you as you walk in the promise of restoration:

" 'I have seen his ways, but I will heal him; I will guide him and restore comfort to him, creating praise on the lips of the mourners in Israel. Peace, peace, to those far and near,' says the LORD. 'And I will heal them' " (Isaiah 57:18–19).

With the promise of restoration ever before you, let its miraculous process begin.

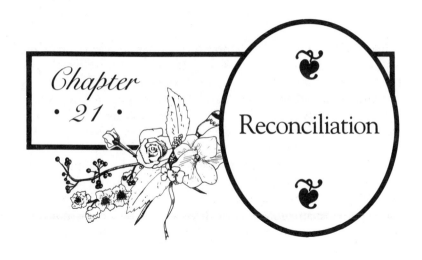

Chapter · 21 ·

Reconciliation

"Blessed are the peacemakers, for they will be called sons of God."

Matthew 5:9

THINK ABOUT IT—God's Word says your sin is forgiven. Your past is settled. There is even a spring returning to your step.

And yet those closest to you may still look at you with eyes filled with pain and distrust. They see a change, and they're grateful for your sake, but—

Could it be that while you have walked on, focused on your own progress, they are somehow stuck—back where the pain began? Could it be that while you are being healed, they are still hurting?

What is wrong with this picture? Maybe you didn't ruin their lives—but perhaps you ruined their plans or ridiculed their goals. You may not have broken up a marriage, but did you spoil something sweet and pure in someone's heart?

Moving on to new places and new people is not the answer—reconciliation is. In previous sections of this book we have focused on repentance and the inner work required for a new start. Now we are ready for further steps.

In the wake of your life and mine, there often lies damage and debris. If our relationship with God has suffered, the people important to us will have suffered, too. Thankfully, with some effort on our part, relationships can be restored.

David's prayer to God was, "Please don't leave me." That may be your request, too—and not only of God, but of a spouse, family member, or friend.

Rebuilding relationships takes time, and a renewed willingness to be vulnerable. It takes time to rebuild trust. Sometimes love has to be rekindled, and a new foundation for it established. Damaged relationships can be restored—but only through a process of reconciliation. God can restore you, and your *relationships* as well.

Reconciliation is a theme close to God's own heart. Listen to these words of Paul:

"All this is from God, who reconciled us to himself through Christ and gave us the ministry of reconciliation: that God was reconciling the world to himself in Christ, not counting men's sins against them. And he has committed to us the message of reconciliation. We are therefore Christ's ambassadors, as though God were making his appeal through us. We implore you on Christ's behalf: Be reconciled to God" (2 Corinthians 5:18–20).

Our first need, then, is to be reconciled to God. Through the promises of God, we find confidence to come close to Him once again.

As the writer of Hebrews says:

"Let us draw near to God with a sincere heart in full assurance of faith, having our hearts sprinkled to cleanse us from a guilty conscience and having our bodies washed with pure water" (Hebrews 10:22).

Now, secure in His love, refreshed by His Spirit, we can say with the words of Psalm 17:8, "Hide me in the shadow of your wings."

Imagine that kind of closeness with God! Because of it, we can approach damaged human relationships with new courage.

Many behaviors hurt a relationship—neglect, abandonment, betraying a confidence, criticism, abuse, and manipulation, to name a few.

And though a relationship may not be exactly as it was, lines of communication can be reopened. Trust can be rebuilt. Love can be rediscovered.

Are you interested in the "how to" of reconciliation?

In Matthew, we find these familiar words:

"Therefore, if you are offering your gift at the altar and there remember that your brother has something against you, leave your gift there in front of the altar. First go and be reconciled to your brother, then come and offer your gift" (Matthew 5:23–24).

As important as it is to fulfill our Christian practices of worship, prayer, and other areas of service, restoration of a relationship takes priority here. We must take responsibility for the hurt and pain we may have caused others.

The Matthew 5 reference shows four steps to reconciliation:

1. *Bring your gift*—like a deposit or guarantee that you will be back.

    (This reminds me of when my son had to leave his driver's license as a security deposit on a rented surfboard. The owner of that surfboard had a guarantee that my son would be back—bringing the surfboard with him.)

2. *Leave your gift and go*—that means *you* go.

    Don't wait for the other person to come to you to be reconciled. *You* make the attempt to work out the problem, ask forgiveness, or renew commitment to the relationship.

3. *Return to the altar*—don't forget God at the altar when you are with your brother.

    After the reconciliation, or the attempt at reconciliation, go back to the altar. God is waiting for you.

4. *Offer your gift*—not only what you left there, but the *obedience* you bring back with you.

    The outcome of an attempted reconciliation is not your responsibility. You may not be able to predict or promise a positive response. Leave it with the Lord. All you are asked to do is *try*. We can all do that.

———————

The Bible says, "When a man's ways are pleasing to the Lord, he makes even his enemies live at peace with him" (Proverbs 16:7). In light of this verse, what relationship in your life is in need of reconciliation?

Psalm 34:14 says, "Turn from evil and do good; seek peace and pursue it." What ways can you think of to seek peace with that person?

"If it is possible, as far as it depends on you, live at peace with everyone" (Romans 12:18). What barriers will you face in your attempts at reconciliation?

What things could you do to "live at peace" with someone who is at odds with you?

Are you willing to "make every effort" toward reconciliation?

(Hebrews 12:14). If you are not willing, why not?

1 Peter 3:11 repeats a phrase found in other references in the Bible: "Seek peace and pursue it." *Pursue* is a strong word. It means making a determined effort, even when the first one fails. What could you try next if your first efforts fail?

*"Set your minds on things above, not on earthly things.
For you died, and your life is now hidden with Christ in
God."*

Colossians 3:2

"IS HE DEAD?" the young father asked.

"Yes," the servant replied, "your son is dead."

Tragically, David had to face the reality of the death of
his innocent baby son. He had fasted and prayed and spent
seven long, sleepless nights prostrate on the floor asking God
to heal the little boy. But God said no. When the news of his
son's death arrived, David did something quite unexpected.
He got up, bathed, and put on clean clothes. He went to the
house of the Lord and worshiped. Upon returning home he
asked for something to eat.

The servants were shocked at his strange behavior. Seeing
him beside himself while the child was ill, they were afraid of
what he might do if the child died. Understandably, when
they saw his sudden return to normalcy they were confused.

They even asked him, "Why are you acting this way?
While the child was alive, you fasted and wept, but now that
the child is dead, you get up and eat!" (2 Samuel 12:21).

112

David replied, "While the child was still alive, I fasted and wept. I thought, 'Who knows? The Lord may be gracious to me and let the child live.' But now that he is dead, why should I fast? Can I bring him back again? I will go to him, but he will not return to me" (2 Samuel 12:22).

David had refocused his life.

There are times when we need to refocus. Maybe now is a time for you to refocus your life.

If you have made honest attempts—*every effort* to reconcile a broken relationship, repair a broken promise, or rebuild damaged trust, and it hasn't happened—what then? It's time to go on—time to refocus. Going on sounds so simple, but often it is not that easy, because of the pain that remains.

Like David, you may discover that it's over, and you can't do anything more about a broken relationship. Quite possibly, you have discovered a broken promise you cannot repair. Maybe the reality is that you can never rebuild a damaged trust. There are some things we simply cannot fix.

You may feel that while you have taken several positive steps forward—an irreparable situation has just hurled you several *giant* steps backward. Maybe you feel a sad acceptance, such as David must have felt after seven days and nights of fasting and prayer and sleeping on the floor: worn out, aching all over, hungry, and lonesome for God.

But there comes a time, just as it did for David, when we must go on. I doubt that David went on without pain. But he did change his focus. It's time to seriously consider whether you must change yours.

You may be feeling pain over something that cannot be mended. You may feel you can do nothing *about* the pain. But you can certainly do something *with* the pain. I have, and so can you.

Let the pain be the very thing that motivates you to press closer than ever before to the open, loving, waiting arms of your heavenly Father.

Let the pain energize you. It can motivate you to look at the inner part of you that has not been completely yielded to God. Perhaps your pain has pointed out love that you held in reserve from Him. Quite possibly you were holding a part of your heart in reserve for the relationship you hoped would be restored, but was not.

113

Maybe secrets you have kept have surfaced because of your pain. Or maybe in your case your pain has helped you to identify the times you have taken your own initiative instead of relying on God's strength, help, and power. Perhaps you have prided yourself in being strong and independent, instead of being what you considered to be *weak* and *dependent* on His sufficiency.

By choosing to refocus, you may have to suffer some pain— but you don't have to allow it to destroy you. You can grow through it. While no one goes out and looks for pain, when it comes we can take it and allow it to make us strong.

When we refocus on God there comes a sense of complete *belonging* to Him. It is not the same as presenting ownership of ourselves to God—it is the knowing that He has taken us. It is not my saying, "I belong to God"—it is God saying, "You belong to me!"

It is the difference between having a godly sense of individual worth and the popular concept of building a positive self-image. Because it is based on human relationships, a perceived good self-image can be fickle. Self-image can ebb and flow with the tide of "warm fuzzies" within our human relationships. And worse, when we *fail* in human relationships a positive self-image can actually cease to exist!

We need something more secure. That's why we need to refocus on our individual worth to the One who created us.

No matter how many times we fail in our attempts at reconciliation in human relationships, we can be assured of our relationship with God. Just as human relationships provide the basis for our self-image, our relationship with God determines our individual worth.

You can be secure in His love. It doesn't mean that broken human relationships don't matter anymore, or that we can't be hurt, but rather, that if every meaningful human relationship is destroyed, your relationship to God will still go on.

This incredible faithfulness of God is why you owe it to yourself to let the process of Psalm 51 do its complete work in your heart.

You belong to God, and you can be deeply aware of His constant care. Because He is your loving and patient Savior, let your spirit soak in the security of His love for you.

Remind yourself that this new sense of individual worth is not based on your performance or character—but on His. Your individual worth will not betray you when a friend rejects you—it is eternal. Take it; God wants you to have it.

———

Secure in your newfound sense of *eternal* worth, how can you surrender yourself to God at a deeper level?

At this new point of personal surrender, what broken relationship do you need to give to Him?

Write out a prayer in which you surrender that relationship to Him.

Now, consciously, totally—*belong* to Him!

At a depth never before explored—*experience* the presence of Jesus. In the quiet place where you are, alone with God, remain at least five minutes in silence, drinking in His matchless love.

How would you like to respond to God, to thank Him for His

love and care for you?

After David had been with the Lord and refreshed himself with a meal, he went to comfort Bathsheba. His thoughts first refocused on worship, then focused on the child's mother and her needs. When you leave the place of communion alone with God, is there someone you could go to and encourage or comfort?

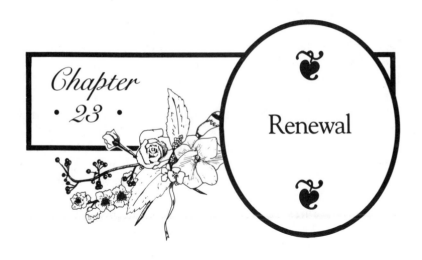

"But those who hope in the LORD will renew their strength. They will soar up on wings like eagles; they will run and not grow weary, they will walk and not be faint."

Isaiah 40:31

"THERE HAS NEVER BEEN a spiritual renewal that did not begin with an acute sense of sin," an evangelist once said.

Through close identification with David—the man, not the king—you have become aware of sin, or faced your sinful self. I did. And with that confrontation we have become acutely aware of our need for renewal.

We have called upon our merciful God, repented, and begun to have the hope of a new heart and a new start—the beginning of a total renewal.

We have found God faithful to His promise in Jeremiah 3:22:

"Return, faithless people; I will cure you of backsliding."

And we have responded: "Yes, we will come to you, for you are the LORD our God."

What a relief! To know that we have a God who forgives— to know that we have a God who understands, and who can heal and help us. He will teach us His ways; He will make us more like himself; He will lead us in the right direction. For He says: "I will heal their waywardness and love them freely, for my anger has turned away from them" (Hosea 14:4). And if that weren't enough He adds these words: "Their sins and lawless acts I will remember no more" (Hebrews 10:17).

In addition to forgiveness, He refreshes us with the promises of His Word: "I will be like the dew to Israel; he will blossom like a lily. Like a cedar of Lebanon he will send down his roots" (Hosea 14:5).

He invigorates us: "His young shoots will grow. His splendor will be like an olive tree, his fragrance like a cedar of Lebanon" (Hosea 14:6).

He reinstates us: "Men will dwell again in his shade. He will flourish like the grain. He will blossom like a vine, and his fame will be like the wine from Lebanon" (Hosea 14:7).

What a loving, compassionate God we serve! Society may expect us to walk in guilt and shame indefinitely, but we no longer conform to what the world says. We have been transformed! Our minds have been renewed by God's Word and our hearts by His mercy. Our lives are changed by His love.

No longer bound by guilt, no longer chained to our past and its shame—we are free!

Free to capture the vision of His majesty. To seize the significance of our salvation. To catch a glimpse of His beauty and the reality of our redemption.

We are renewed.

It is springtime within us. Our spirits are as alive as meadows carpeted with the bright yellow, orange, purple, and raspberry wildflowers of a new season. Hallelujahs want to burst forth from our lips.

Christopher Morley said, "April prepares her green traffic light and the world thinks go."

God has reached down from heaven with a new touch upon our lives—how refreshing! He has pumped new life, His life, into us—how invigorating! He has placed us within His reach and love—fully reinstated! He speaks through His word to us about His plans and purposes for our lives—we are restored! A new beginning lies ahead—what a responsibility!

We are challenged by the words of the great evangelist of

long ago, Charles Finney: "The experience of revival is nothing more than a new beginning of obedience to God."

Responsibilities dreaded before become welcome and revitalizing. We anticipate our quiet times and look forward to prayer times. We approach work with new enthusiasm and play with new joy. We welcome ministry opportunities with sensitivity and compassion.

Renewal provides one-hundred percent of what we need to begin our walk of obedience. It furnishes all the hope we need to persevere in renewed commitment to Jesus.

Obedience now opens the way to new fruitfulness and productivity. It gives new attitudes of promise and possibility to goal setting and makes dreams seem manageable and real. Obedience turns every temptation into an opportunity to grow in greater obedience. It unlocks witnessing opportunities and gives us a firm underfooting during times of life's uncertainties.

Obedience enables us to delight in everyday blessings. With the renewal of the soul comes the revival of the senses. The smell of fresh food is full and rich. The cool, crisp feel of clean sheets on the bed becomes a savored luxury. Sunshine is brighter. Birds sing louder. An orange tastes "orangier." Life is wonderful! This is the experience of renewal—and praise be to our matchless God, we can experience it for ourselves.

List some ways in which you are renewed:

If you are renewed, how do you see your responsibilities before God differently than you did before your renewal?

With the promise of continued restoration, how do you see your inner life changing?

How do you see your outer life changing?

List some words of praise you would like to express to God.

Chapter
• 24 •

Reconfirmation

"Come near to God and he will come near to you."
James 4:8

HOW MANY TIMES have you been given the "silent treatment" or "cold shoulder" when something you've done or said has upset another? We may become so accustomed to this kind of abusive treatment that we expect the same of God. We are convinced that we deserve His silence. And when communication closes down between us we assume it is God who has distanced himself from us, rather than distancing ourselves from Him.

But now we know that He has not turned His back on us, nor has He withheld His Spirit from us.

He is not like us—nor like anyone we have ever known or trusted before. He is the One "who tends his flock like a shepherd: He gathers the lambs in his arms and carries them close to his heart" (Isaiah 40:11).

We are the ones who pull away.

In our pattern of non-communicating, we shut Him out. We are so accustomed to human relationships where issues are not resolved that we tend to settle for cooled emotions rather than full restoration and resolution. When we have sinned, we have given God space and time to "cool off." In fact, we have given Him so much space we may feel that the distance is too wide to close again.

But things are different now. We no longer need to pull away from God. The gentle Shepherd who never gives anyone a cold shoulder is always there, waiting to restore us to His presence. We have rediscovered our heavenly Father, the God of love. We have returned to His presence, to be changed by His mercy and grace.

It is in His presence that we also discover the reconfir-mation of His purpose for our lives, His calling into ministry, and receive direction on how to proceed. Where once we acted on impulse and random effort, we have now discovered *divine purpose.*

From the very beginning of the Bible, we see that God does indeed operate with a purpose:

"But I have raised you up for this very purpose, that I might show you my power and that my name might be proclaimed in all the earth" (Exodus 9:16).

The words that caused fear in Pharaoh's heart are the very words we thrive on.

"My food," said Jesus, "is to do the will of him who sent me and to finish his work" (John 4:34).

Jesus knew His purpose on earth. You and I can know it, too.

Paul had a specific goal:

"Brothers, I do not consider myself yet to have taken hold of the goal. But one thing I do: forgetting what is behind and straining toward what is ahead, I press on toward the goal to win the prize for which God has called me heavenward in Christ Jesus" (Philippians 3:13).

What is the goal of your life? What part of God's work and kingdom has He assigned to you?

"As a prisoner for the Lord, then, I urge you to live a life worthy of the calling you have received" (Ephesians 4:1).

What is your calling? Once you recapture God's purpose for your life, you become a purposeful Christian, reclaiming your sense of destiny.

"Be all the more eager to make your calling and election sure" (2 Peter 1:10).

How in the world do you do that? By taking the following brave steps:

1. In prayer, go to the Lord and *volunteer:*

"Then I heard the voice of the Lord saying, 'Whom shall I send? And who will go for us?' And I said, 'Here am I. Send me!' " (Isaiah 6:8)

2. Then, like Elisha, within the context of your daily life and service, wait for His anointing:

"So Elijah went from there and found Elisha son of Shaphat. He was plowing with twelve yoke of oxen, and he himself was driving the twelfth pair. Elijah went up to him and threw his cloak around him" (1 Kings 19:19).

3. Leave behind whatever He tells you to leave:

"The LORD had said to Abram, 'Leave your country, your people and your father's household . . .' "

4. Go where *He* sends you:

" . . . and go to the land I will show you' " (Genesis 12:1).

5. Go in the strength He gives you:

"The LORD turned to him and said, 'Go in the strength you have and save Israel out of Midian's hand. Am I not sending you?' " (Judges 6:14)

6. Stand tall in your call:

"Now get up and stand on your feet. I have appeared to you to appoint you as a servant and as a witness of what you have seen of me and what I will show you" (Acts 26:16).

David's prayer of Psalm 51:11 must be your prayer as you are reconfirmed for His service:

"Do not cast me from your presence or take your Holy Spirit from me."

What is God calling you to do? Has He already gifted you with hospitality, social service, or serving the church in some way? Has He called you to intercession, leadership, or teaching? Maybe you have heard Him call you to missionary work or writing. Perhaps it is speaking, music, or counseling. Whatever it is, let those callings and gifts be reconfirmed in you. You've come so far, and full restoration is just ahead.

———————

What might God give you to do today that you are fully capable of and prepared for?

If God asks you to do something, then it is "ministry." His purpose for you begins with whatever He puts in your hand. What is in your hand, within your reach and power? Choose to do something for Him today. Here are some suggestions:

Send a card or note of appreciation to someone.

Call a friend who has been down or lonely.

Offer to take someone's turn at their post of duty at your church.

Offer to answer the phone at your church one afternoon this week.

Visit a nursing home and find someone who needs a loving touch or kind word.

How will you determine if what you have chosen to do is really God's will for you and not just a suggestion you picked up? (Review the six brave steps outlined in this chapter.)

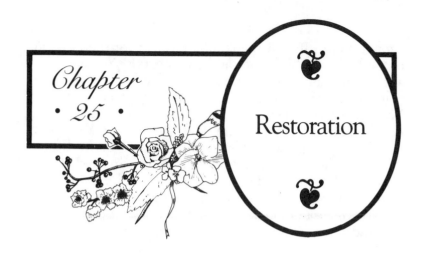

Chapter · 25 ·

Restoration

"Restore to me the joy of your salvation and grant me a willing spirit, to sustain me."

Psalm 51:12

DO YOU LOVE the promise of being restored?

Restoration is not "re-qualifying for ministry," but it does mean being more prepared for ministry than ever before. It is as much preparation for the future as it is being rescued from the past.

Full restoration prepares us to overcome when past failures and disappointments come back to mind, tempting us to discouragement and regret.

Choose to no longer live in the pain of the past. Choose to experience the full joy of Christ's complete sacrifice, and decide to call upon the Lord:

"Restore to me the joy of your salvation and grant me a willing spirit, to sustain me" (Psalm 51:12).

During the process of your restoration, it is crucial that your joy be based not on your own perfection but on His.

It is right and good that you desire all God has for you— to welcome His blessings and be enthralled with His presence. It's all right to count on His protective intervention in your behalf, and to live in thankful enjoyment for the provisions of food, shelter, clothing, and good health. You are free to ask His blessing upon your home and family, to be present in your worship, and to multiply the offerings you bring to Him. You can be confident that He welcomes your petitions and requests, and can expect Him to answer your prayers.

When you are sick, draw from His provision for healing. When confused, ask for His answers. When in need of direction, ask Him to guide you. Are you lonely? Receive His companionship. Even in death He is the Victor.

You *can* ask of God.

And when He asks something of you, be ready to respond.

Many are eager to do something useful for God, but rebel at the thought of preparing for it. He requires a willing spirit and the discipline of preparation.

Returning to service without full restoration and complete preparation may get you right back to where you were at the beginning:

"Are you so foolish? After beginning with the Spirit, are you now trying to attain your goal by human effort? Have you suffered so much for nothing—as if it really was for nothing?" (Galatians 3:3–4).

David knew that only God could do the work needed to grant him a willing spirit, to sustain him. David did not want a quick fix, he had long-range goals for serving God. So must we.

Getting ready for more ministry is the final phase of the restoration process. Following a time of spiritual preparation, there comes the practical side of doing what one has been called to do.

The Bible gives several examples of the importance of preparation:

There can be no water until the ditches are dug:

"This is what the LORD says: Make this valley full of ditches. For this is what the LORD says: You will see neither wind nor rain, yet this valley will be filled with water, and you, your cattle and your other animals will drink" (2 Kings 3:16–17).

No oil until the vessels have been gathered:

"Elisha said, 'Go around and ask all your neighbors for empty jars. Don't ask for just a few. Then go inside and shut the door behind you and your sons. Pour oil into all the jars, and as each is filled, put it to one side' " (2 Kings 4:3).

No harvest until the ground is broken up:

"Sow for yourselves righteousness, reap the fruit of unfailing love, and break up your unplowed ground; for it is time to seek the LORD, until he comes and showers righteousness on you" (Hosea 10:12).

Preparation takes time: time to make certain the calling of God, time to learn and to reflect on experiences and their lessons. Time to read books, take classes, or attend seminars that may help to prepare us for service.

Some will want to place themselves under the training and guidance of a mentor who will hold them accountable during their time of preparation. Some will want to see a counselor or pastor for the same reasons.

Many times restoration begins with small ministry opportunities under the guidance of those who are equally committed to your restoration.

You may not be ready to be on your own yet, but you will be, and you are closer to full responsibility than you were.

The time will come when you will serve in your full capacity with a fresh anointing of God's Holy Spirit. And you'll be glad you didn't rush into something as important as your service to God.

———

What do you think God is asking you to do?

What kind of preparation seems wise to you?

Is there something that tempts you to rush the process of preparation?

How will your life be different when you are fully restored?

Are you willing to trust God for the timing of your ministry?

Are you willing to wait on Him and prepare?

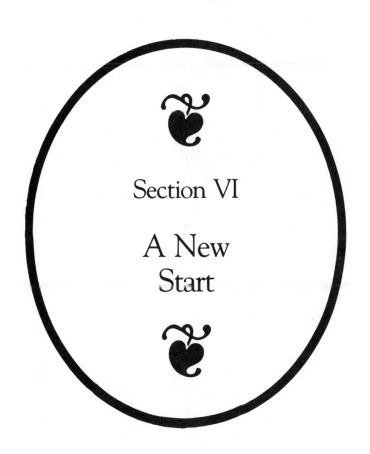

Section VI

A New
Start

T hen I will teach transgressors your ways,
    and sinners will turn back to you.
Save me from bloodguilt, O God,
    the God who saves me,
    and my tongue will sing of your righteousness.
O Lord, open my lips,
    and my mouth will sing your praise.

PSALM 51:13–14

IN RECENT TIMES Christians have had to face the fact that leaders, even strong Christian leaders, can fail. We look at the damage caused by their failures and wonder if there is hope for us.

Not only is there hope, but there is promise of a new life and ministry after failure. If this were not true churches would be without members and ministries would be without leadership. All of us are capable of failure, and we all fail in one capacity or another. How the failure is handled is what determines our future.

David failed. But after the failure he went on to accomplish great things. Psalm 51 is his prayer of repentance—his turning point. In it we see him begin to refocus on something other than himself and his past.

Verse thirteen of Psalm 51 begins with *then*. This indicates a *before*—pre-mercy, pre-repentance, and pre-change. Before there was pain instead of fruitfulness, but God met David in a miraculous way. He didn't leave him in his pre-change condition. Our gracious Father-God coaxed David through the process and into the promise of restoration. He didn't leave him with his past, but gave him a future.

After David experienced God's mercy; after he knew God's compassion; after he realized the full extent of the hurt caused by his sinful actions; after he learned truth in his inner being and was restored to joy and gladness; after he received a new heart and was once again secure in the Holy Spirit's presence—*then*, and only then did David experience a new concern for others—a new spiritual service.

If you have wondered if God can ever use you again, the answer is a resounding *yes!* And when God uses you, it will be a delightful, fruitful, and purposeful ministry.

Because ministry can bring extra pressure, exposure to temptation, and assault of the enemy, it is essential that your past be fully exposed to God, that your heart be fully open to Him, and your mind be clear of condemnation. That is why it is important to give God time and the freedom to help you fully heal from your failure and pain. God is more interested in the *minister* than the ministry.

Often those who have had difficulties with sin find that their service to God *after* restoration is very different than their service before. That is why it is important not to rush into service before God has done a deep work within. Restoration will bring less tendency to legalism, more compassion for others, and more tolerance of the shortcomings and failings of those on the road to recovery. There is a new identification with pain and regret, and more tenderness toward those who have suffered in a like manner. God takes what has been ruined and "picks up the pieces." He restores, rebuilds, makes us more fully alive than ever before.

Yes, God can use you, my friend. Because of Jesus, no mistake is too great that we cannot be forgiven and restored.

If you have used your failure as an excuse not to follow the call of God, I trust by now that has been stripped away.

It is a new beginning, different from the past. This is not the old life—it is a new start.

Chapter · 26 ·

Beginning Anew

"Save me from bloodguilt, O God, the God who saves me, and my tongue will sing of your righteousness."

PSALM 51:14

DAVID PRAYED, "Save me from bloodguilt." David had committed murder and then asked forgiveness, yet he prays again to be saved from the guilt of his crime.

How could David pray such a prayer? It is the prayer of a new man. He had taken another's life; he had experienced forgiveness. Now his prayer is based not on the past but on the present, with an eye toward a hopeful future. It is the prayer of a man with a *new* heart. He wanted new direction, a new attitude, and a new commitment to live a life free from the guilt and pain of sin.

In his book, *Finding the Heart to Go On*, Lynn Anderson writes these words:

> Things began changing for David that day. Securely back in dialogue with God, he had manfully recovered his integrity. His dignity returned also, along with his security. Once more he stood tall.

We too can stand tall, in integrity and with dignity.

Beginning anew is not the same as starting over. Perhaps an analogy can express this concept best.

In the 1992 Winter Olympic games, every medal winner in the women's figure skating competition fell in her final program. It made history.

Each competitor approached her routine having done it perfectly hundreds of times before that night. But under the pressure of competition and the weariness of the strenuous events, slips and misjudgments happened. In the face of those errors it was the trained athletes who fell—but it was the champions who got up and went on. They could not re-do the whole program, but only pick up where they fell. They were champions because they knew how to get up and go on unshaken.

Silver medalist Midori Ito said it best: "I had a program to finish; I had to put my mistake behind me."

Lynn Anderson also writes:

> When a man has truly faced his mistakes and knows the forgiveness of God, he is secure in God—but only in God. Then something about him often attracts the loyalty, admiration, and love of the courageous and penitent people. There is no need to wallow in our mire all of our days, nor to rob the world of our gifts because of past failures. We are too hard on ourselves.

Like the Olympic medalists, you too have a program to finish. Like a champion, you must get up and get on with it.

I see my salvation as the time I accepted the sacrifice Christ made on the cross for my sin. Then all the mistakes, all the errors in judgment, all the occurrences of sin in my life since then have been the times when I have learned to *apply* what I accepted so many years ago.

Let the cross represent life and a new beginning for you—new life when you accepted Jesus as your Savior, and a new beginning as you apply all you've learned until now.

You can live the life; you can finish the course. Accept as your own personal promise Ezekiel 11:19:

"I will give them an undivided heart and put a new spirit in them; I will remove from them their heart of stone and give them a heart of flesh."

Think of God, saying about you:

"For this son of mine was dead and is alive again; he was lost and is found" (Luke 15:24).

––––––––––

How are you choosing to go on?

What new attitudes do you have?

What is your new direction?

In what ways do you need to forgive yourself?

What new commitments have you made?

What new possibilities do you see?

What opportunities for Christian service are open to you now (at your church, at your place of work, in your neighborhood, in your home)?

Chapter
· 27 ·

The Out of and Into Principle

"But he brought us out from there to bring us in and give us the land that he promised on oath to our forefathers."

Deuteronomy 6:23

IT IS IMPORTANT TO LOOK at Psalm 51 in the context of David's life.

Miserable and in crisis, David cried out to God. Early in the prayer David says, "For I know my transgressions, and my sin is always before me" (verse 3). Then later he says, "Then I will teach transgressors your ways, and sinners will turn back to you" (verse 13). What a change—not only in David's prayer, but in *him*.

David had come a long way. And his path produced within him a process based on the promise of restoration. David is a good example of what I call the "out of and into" principle.

For several years I have marked scriptures that contain this principle. Take a few minutes to meditate on those listed here:

Out of sin, into purity:

"If we confess our sins, he is faithful and just and will forgive us our sins and purify us from all unrighteousness" (1 John 1:9).

Out of self, into submission:

"For we know that our old self was crucified with him so that the body of sin might be done away with, that we should no longer be slaves to sin" (Romans 6:6).

"I have been crucified with Christ and I no longer live, but Christ lives in me. The life I live in the body, I live by faith in the Son of God, who loved me and gave himself for me" (Galatians 2:20).

Out of shame, into cleansing:

" 'Come now, let us reason together,' says the LORD. 'Though your sins are like scarlet, they shall be as white as snow; though they are as red as crimson, they shall be like wool. If you are willing and obedient, you will eat the best from the land' " (Isaiah 1:18–19).

Out of ruin, into relationship:

"Here I am! I stand at the door and knock. If anyone hears my voice and opens the door, I will come in and eat with him, and he with me" (Revelation 3:20).

Out of regret, into release:

" 'Return faithless people; I will cure you of backsliding. Yes, we will come to you, for you are the LORD our God' " (Jeremiah 3:22).

Out of despair, into celebration:

"I tell you that in the same way there will be more rejoicing in heaven over one sinner who repents than over ninety-nine righteous persons who do not need to repent" (Luke 15:7).

Out of battle, into blessing:

"See, I am setting before you today a blessing and a curse—the blessing if you obey the commands of the LORD your God that I am giving you today; the curse if you disobey the commands of the LORD your God and turn from the way that I command you today by following other gods, which you have not known" (Deuteronomy 11:26–28).

It is exciting to look into the promises of God and find His answers to our greatest needs. The samples provided are only a few. Find more for yourself through your own study of His Word!

What is a new start if it is not coming out of something you want to leave behind and into the new things you desire?

In the past, what are some of the situations you have asked God to remove you from or deliver you from?

As you begin afresh, what are some areas you would have Him lead you into?

Finish the following statements:

Out of my cave of _____ , on with my call of _____ .

Out of my pit of _____ , on with my purpose of _____ .

What application to your own life can you make from the following?

Out of depression, into new dignity:

Out of self-pity, into His promises:

Today is the second day of your new start. How is it going so far?

Maybe you once thought you didn't deserve a second chance, or felt disqualified—even tossed aside—never to be used again by the Lord. But here you are, fully involved and making your new start. Do you think you are as committed to your new start as He is?

Chapter · 28 ·

God's Agenda— My Agenda

"I desire to do your will, O my God; your law is within my heart."

Psalm 40:8

A NEW START doesn't begin with fanfare, nor does it begin with a burst of enthusiasm. It begins with the discipline of seeking the Lord, walking in His Word and waiting for His direction.

A new start often means taking risks—for me it was the risk of being misunderstood.

Once, while going through a personal crisis, I said something that was wrongly interpreted. Then it was repeated, causing misunderstanding and pain. I wanted to go directly to the person involved and defend myself. I was hurting, she was hurting, and people who loved us both were trying to help. Things were blown out of proportion.

It seemed the more we all tried to fix it, the worse the situation became—month after month.

Finally, I found a private place to be alone and sobbed out my confusion and frustration to God.

Be still, He seemed to whisper to my heart. *Just be quiet. Be quiet? Stop talking? If I don't straighten it out who will?*

141

I experienced a moment of panic. I am such a fixer that to stop trying to fix it meant to me that the relationships would always be broken. I experienced fear. Fear that the situation might never be resolved. I had to be willing to let the misunderstanding go uncorrected and knew that as a result I could possibly lose a friend forever.

But as I sat alone in God's presence I surrendered to Him. For the first time in more than a year I experienced peace.

Silence can be the pathway to peace and freedom.

Sometime later I learned that to be close-mouthed about a particular incident did not mean clamming up completely. It was only when I stopped talking to my friends about my pain and regrets that I found God talking to me about those same important issues.

Many morning quiet times were spent in stillness before the Lord. In a notebook I listed three items:

1. Scriptural principles I have violated.
2. Scriptural principles I need to obey for cleansing and healing.
3. Scriptural principles I need to apply to my life for growth.

I didn't share these insights with anyone. I was learning to surrender and to be silent—but I was also learning something else: the difference between my agenda and God's agenda.

I had waited on God before. At least I thought I had. But in looking back, I saw that I held up my end of the conversation quite well, and when it came time for Him to speak to me—well, I was already late for work; the family needed attention; or: Isn't this the day the dog goes to the vet?

You too have had one-sided conversations with the Lord. Can you identify with similar distractions?

I'm sure I have had conversations with people who were only waiting for me to finish talking so they could speak. They were probably not listening, but thinking about what they would say when I shut up. Some have patiently given details of their concerns to me, but when I tried to respond they were a million miles away before I got a complete sentence out. Sadly, my prayer life was much like that.

But it has changed.

I no longer only bring God lists of requests, telling Him how to do His job. I have learned to listen. I listen for His voice, wait for His agenda, instead of just presenting Him with mine.

I have learned to seek the Lord. Not His love, His wisdom, His will alone—but Him. When I do that, I am showered with His love, His wisdom, and a knowledge of His will.

Then I am secure in asking Him specific questions concerning direction, method, timing, and insight.

The new start comes as we learn about God's agenda—His will. Without that, we are apt to find ourselves in still another mess of self-directed, self-motivated, and self-sustained works.

Let us abandon our own agendas for God's, and embrace the discipline of waiting until He reveals His particular plan for us. Pray with the psalmist:

"Teach me your way, O LORD, and I will walk in your truth; give me an undivided heart, that I may fear your name" (Psalm 86:11).

Let us go forward, fully trained for battle, singing a new song to God, assured of His victory. Let this be our song as we leave our place of private consultation with our King:

"Sing to the LORD a new song; sing to the LORD, all the earth. Sing to the LORD, praise his name; proclaim his salvation day after day. Declare his glory among the nations, his marvelous deeds among all peoples. For great is the LORD and most worthy of praise; he is to be feared above all gods" (Psalm 96:1–4).

———

Have you ever been afraid to fully trust God to reveal His agenda for you—thinking He might not have one?

Which thought frightens you the most? Why?
He might not use me.
He might use me.

143

If you were to fully accept God's agenda for your life and lay aside your own, what would you have to give up?

What plans do you think you could keep?

A New Heart— A New Start

"For we are God's workmanship, created in Christ Jesus to do good works, which God prepared in advance for us to do."

Ephesians 2:10

DAVID IS A DIFFERENT MAN than the one we saw in prayer at the beginning of Psalm 51. (He is a man who can identify with those who fail, and with those who suffer the consequences.)

In much the same way, we are different than when we started the study of David's prayer. If we have allowed the application in our lives of what we have learned in this study, we can identify with and touch others at a deeper level than we could before. I would like to illustrate this difference with a personal experience:

A few years ago I faced radical surgery. My situation was a matter of life or death, and the physical trauma was compounded by emotional and spiritual trauma. Every area of my life was at stake—personally and professionally. I was in deep trouble.

When the doctor came into my room to see me the night before surgery, he said many comforting things, and then he prayed with me.

One of the things he said was this: "I have studied your case thoroughly and am well aware of what you need done in this surgery. I have studied the intestinal system at length, and have performed many surgeries on others with good success."

I waited for him to say something special to me that would be the key to my confidence.

But he went on, "I know this surgery inside and out and know exactly how I will begin, what I will do, and how I will finish. I know everything there is to know about this operation."

"Have you ever had the surgery?" I asked.

"No," he said, "I haven't."

"Then, doctor," I said quietly, "you don't know how it feels, do you?"

If only he could have said, "I know how it feels," it would have added a whole new dimension of meaning and credibility to his words of comfort and encouragement. But of course he couldn't say that, because he had never experienced it as the patient.

David brings meaning and credibility to his statement, "Then I will teach transgressors your ways, and sinners will turn back to you" (Psalm 51:13), because he had experienced the ways of God and His great mercy and compassion toward him in spite of his sin.

This is the same new dimension our service will have. We will see people with new eyes, and have a deeper understanding of those who are hurting because of their failures. We will counsel with new tolerance and patience. We will love where before we may have judged. We will bring hope to those who have none.

To have this kind of effectiveness requires that we open ourselves to a deeper vulnerability. It means that we will hurt with others, feel their pain—and in that openness, allow others to feel our pain.

It doesn't mean a lifelong rehearsal of the details of our sins and shortcomings. But it does mean that we will no longer hide our scars behind screens of perfection and masks of pretense. We may not speak of the sordid details of our past, but we will speak of healing and hope with the voice of experience

146

and the compassion of one who has been there.

Many say they *must* write a book about their experiences. For whom would you write the book? What is your motivation? Are you motivated by what God did for you and your need to share it, or by what you feel God wants to do for others through you? The first means you will probably share the details of your past experiences; the second means you will share the *changed person* with others. Not every story needs to be told.

———————

If an unbeliever crossed your path today in search of hope and an understanding heart, how would he or she find yours?

Are you willing to let God use the lessons you have learned to deepen your capacity for compassion, tolerance, and love?

Have you already seen expressions of your new depth in dealing with others? In what ways?

When seeking to give hope to someone who is hurting and discouraged, are you more apt to share your mistakes in detail, or only that you have made mistakes and how God has helped you overcome them and deal with them?

Which is most helpful in your estimation—giving the details, or sharing God's solution?

What does having a new heart mean to you?

What does having a new start mean to you?

How are they related?

*"And we pray this in order that you may live a life
worthy of the Lord and may please him in every way:
bearing fruit in every good work, growing in the
knowledge of God, being strengthened with all power
according to his glorious might so that you may have great
endurance and patience, and joyfully giving thanks to the
Father, who has qualified you to share in the inheritance
of the saints in the kingdom of light.
For he has rescued us from the dominion of darkness and
brought us into the kingdom of the Son he loves, in whom
we have redemption, the forgiveness of sins."*

Colossians 1:10–14

GOD WILL HEAL THE HURT. God will take away regret
and shame. Life will return to normal again, if we allow Him
to heal and deliver us.

We can walk in complete freedom from our past. God
desires that we do. Listen to the promise of Acts 3:19:

"Repent, then, and turn to God, so that your sins may be
wiped out, that times of refreshing may come from the Lord."

We have taken some important steps in this study:

1. We have confessed sin.

2. We have confronted issues.
3. We have surrendered to God.
4. We have submitted to His cleansing.
5. We have embraced the challenge of change.

We will be tempted to drag the past back into the present. But we must go on with life—our new life.

Rather than serve God because of guilt, we serve Him because of love. Our offerings are from a pure heart and given with clean hands, no longer tainted with sin and shame.

We have changed from the inside out, and that change is making an impact on our lives. It should begin to make an impact on those around us.

According to Romans 12:1, in view of God's mercy we are to offer our bodies as living sacrifices, holy and pleasing to God as a spiritual act of worship.

And in keeping with Hebrews 13:15, 16, we are to continually offer to God a sacrifice of praise, the fruit of lips that confess His name. Finally we are free to do good and to share with others, knowing that God is pleased with our sacrifice.

We have become "like living stones . . . built into a spiritual house to be a holy priesthood, offering spiritual sacrifices acceptable to God through Jesus Christ" (1 Peter 2:5).

We have stopped thinking in terms of our own merit—or disqualification because of what we have done in the past. We have come to the full realization that we are who we are becoming because of Jesus and what He has done.

We are a people with a future—not spiritual nomads or wanderers, but a people of purpose and destiny.

The past is over. The future stretches out before us full of promise and possibility.

We are changed people—new people. Not avoiding decisions that must be made, nor running from responsibility because of the mistakes and failures in our past, we look toward a future based on a newness of heart created in us by God.

No longer haunted by the past, we are free to choose—to make new commitments and follow new direction. In our freedom we set new standards and find new strength by which to live. Experience gives wisdom; God gives a new heart. Our past mistakes have taught us some valuable lessons, but God has given us a new life.

Let us choose not to turn back, nor turn away from all that God has for us. Let us choose to find the strength in Him to face the future and to go on.

What difference does basing decisions on the present and on the future rather than on the past make for you?

What "new start" changes have been put into effect in your life already?

What new strength do you feel you have to face new challenges?

REVIEW

What have I put behind me during this study?

What excuses have I used not to be used of God?

What failure have I experienced that I consider too much for God to forgive?

By what authority have I held my shortcomings higher than God's ability to cleanse and use me?

Throughout this study, what are three of the most important issues that have surfaced in my relationship with Jesus Christ:

1. _____

2. _____

3. _____

These are my goals at the beginning of my "new start":

   1. I choose to be more open to God in these areas:

   2. I am learning to trust God more with the following things about myself:

3. My joy is now based on:

4. I see the following changes taking place within me:

5. Some areas that need more work are:

6. The promises that encourage me now are:

7. Other thoughts and prayers concerning this study are:

GROUP GUIDELINES SUGGESTIONS

As mentioned at the beginning of this book, if this study is used in a group setting, members should study the five entries of each section throughout the week in preparation for discussion at the weekly meeting. In this way, the material is covered in six weeks. A group may decide to spend more or less time on a given section depending on the needs of the participants. Discussion questions are included at the end of these leader's notes.

A good general group approach to this study is one of personal investigation and shared responses. Discussion questions will help bring out even more insight into application for personal growth.

In the course of covering the material, some very personal areas of a participant's life may be exposed or brought to mind. A leader should not expect, or force, everyone to participate each time. Do encourage even the slightest participation with affirmative comments, regardless of the contribution.

Because this is a responsive study, there are no wrong answers. The nature of the study tends to get to the heart of many emotional issues. Some people in your group may desperately need a listening ear, and a correction from you may discourage them from participating in the discussion, or even keep them from attending the study again. Allow the Holy Spirit to do the correcting, and a deep work of patience and sensitivity in you.

If an individual monopolizes the conversation or goes off on a tangent, very carefully approach that person afterward and ask if you can be of help individually. There may be times during the study when a person may genuinely come to a breakthrough, and will draw the attention of the group to herself and her needs entirely. That would be the exception, however, not the rule.

If someone in your group asks a question, don't take the responsibility upon yourself to have the sole answer. Allow others in the group to contribute, and let your answer be given last.

There are three basic rules that you should strive to keep without fail:

1. *Start and end the study at the time previously arranged and agreed upon.*

Everyone is busy. Set your meeting times and stick to them. One and a half hours generally works well for evening groups; daytime groups may wish to meet for a little longer. Actual study discussion should only take a portion of that time. Fellowship and sharing prayer requests helps develop strong bonds within your group. Make time for that to happen.

2. *Begin and end with prayer.*

The opening prayer can be a simple offering by one person asking God's blessing on your time together. You may feel the need in your group to have additional time for prayer concerns or needs of the group. (One effective way to handle this is to have everyone write down the name of the person they are concerned for and a very brief statement about the need on a small piece of paper. The slips are put into a basket and re-distributed to the group. Each person then offers a sentence prayer concerning the request they have drawn from the basket.) Closing prayers should be centered around the needs that have arisen related to the study and discussion. Bring the meeting to a close with your own prayer.

3. *Involve everyone.*

Many of the issues covered in this study are very personal. Depending upon the amount of abuse and misunderstanding your group members have experienced, some may not be ready to discuss the issues they are presently dealing with. However, during the fellowship time, the time of praying for others, and the ongoing study, seek to build trust and encourage them to open their heart and share with the group. Find a way to involve even the most reserved person in a way that is comfortable and safe for her.

Discussion times can be rich and rewarding for everyone. That is, everyone who gets to share and discuss. The size of the group somewhat determines the opportunities for sharing. A group of six members is ideal, but it can work with as many as ten. When the group reaches ten, consider the advantages of dividing into smaller groups of three of four for the sharing and discussion time.

Discussion Questions

Orientation—Introduction

You may find it helpful to have an orientation meeting before you begin the study of this book. Such a meeting will allow members of the group to have opportunity to look over the book and to prepare for the first discussion and sharing time.

The following questions will help your group members get off to a good start, and to help them to understand what is expected to be accomplished in the study.

1. Many people have difficulty fitting a daily quiet time into their routines. What are some of the things you have tried? What are some of the ways that have worked for you, and what are some ways that did not work?
2. Everyone experiences times in their lives when they feel the need to start over to one degree or another—to make a new beginning. What are some of the times when that might occur?
3. When a person reads a book or embarks on a new study, not every illustration or example exactly fits his or her particular situation, and yet may be helpful in some way.

Why do you think this is true?
4. What are some of your expectations with regard to this study?

Assignment

Everyone should first read *How to Use This Book* at the beginning of the book. Each day for five days before we meet again, read and respond to each of the devotional studies in Section I, entitled MERCY. (Before each meeting, members should read and study the five entries for the section to be discussed at the next meeting.)*

Section I: Mercy

To begin the first study, read together the introduction, and then use the following questions for discussion:

1. What chance would any of us have without God's mercy? How would a lack of His mercy affect how we relate to Him?
2. We live in a world that, in general, is not merciful. Perhaps someone would be willing to share a personal example or experience in which they found mercy was lacking.
3. Are you more aware of "mercy killers" now? In what ways?
4. Neva shared her personal experience with a nurse who at first neglected to show kindness to her. Does someone have a similar experience to share? Have any of you ever been in the position where you did not show kindness to someone?
5. Does thinking of mercy as evidence of God's authority change your view of God? Of His authority?
6. Will someone explain the difference between Neva's definitions of lovingkindness and compassion in Chapter Five?
7. When we accept God's offer of friendship, what changes

---

*The above group guidelines are based on standard group dynamic concepts as well as the models found in the *Lifeguide Bible Studies*, IVP; *Leading Bible Discussions* by James F. Nyquist and Jack Kuhatschek, IVP; Aglow International Bible Studies; and Overeaters Victorious Leader's Guidelines.

occur in our hearts? What changes occur in our attitudes toward others? Toward ourselves?

_____

Section II: Encounter With Power

1. Have you ever thought that your weaknesses are really your strengths? Explain. Give examples.
2. How does it feel to finally come to the end of yourself?
3. Share with the group an experience you have had with the power of confession.
4. Why is it easier to confess what we have done than what we are?
5. Why is it sometimes wise to keep the details of our past private from other people?
6. Can a person be open and transparent with God while maintaining privacy with people? Discuss.
7. How is it possible that the truth of our painful past can bring us relief?

_____

Section III: A New Heart

Read together the introduction.

This particular discussion could be threatening to someone who has suffered some kind of abuse during childhood. When speaking about the concept of self-disclosure, keep the discussion in general terms to avoid forcing anyone who is not ready to share into revealing secrets about her past. Respect the privacy of the individuals in your group and set the boundaries before you begin this discussion.

1. Do most people have a secret place within their heart—a heart of hearts so to speak?
2. What do you think most people might keep in that secret place?
3. Which emotion would be most likely to reveal itself when one considers opening the inner heart to the Lord?
4. Which is easier for you—to deal with issues, or deal with yourself and your attitudes?

5. How do you feel when you attend a church service after a fight with your spouse or another family member?
6. What is the difference between conviction and condemnation?
7. Jesus doesn't go around or through our barriers; He removes them. What does that mean to you?
8. David prayed, "Create in me a pure heart." If we pray that prayer, what kind of hope should it inspire in us?

Section IV: A Steadfast Spirit

Read together the introduction.
1. How many can share experiences in which you didn't feel as if you belonged?
2. In spite of your past—whatever *you* have done; whatever has been done *to* you—God says you are clean, if you have indeed asked Him to cleanse you. What difference does that make to you?
3. What difference should being free from God's judgment make in our relationships with others?
4. What emotional difference is there between saying "God loves me" and "God likes me"?
5. What creative way did you find to celebrate the end of your mourning this week?

Section V: Restoration

Read together the introduction.
1. In what ways have you avoided reconciliation?
2. Is there an example from your own experience that you would use to encourage someone else to reconcile to another?
3. Is every broken relationship meant to be restored? Give some examples of when it is best to simply leave the broken relationship in God's hands.
4. Have there been times when it has been apparent that you should refocus and go on with your life without seeing the

resolution of a problem or reconciliation of a relationship?
5. Was it difficult for you to be silent for five minutes and allow yourself to bask in God's presence? If it was, why do you think so?
6. In what ways are you seeing renewal, and what impact is that having in your life?
7. How has God reconfirmed something about His will for your life this week?
8. Is God speaking to anyone about preparation for ministry? Be specific.

———

Section VI: A New Start

Read together the introduction.
1. This is the time to begin anew. How are you choosing to effect this new beginning?
2. What excuses are you still using to avoid a new, fresh start?
3. What new commitments have you made?
4. What new possibilities do you see?
5. Neva defines a new start as *coming out* of something you want to leave behind and *into* something new with God's help. In the past, what are some of the situations you have asked God to take you *out* of? Now, in your new start, what are some areas you would like Him to lead you *into*?
6. What have you learned about the difference between God's agenda and your own agenda?
7. How are you different than when you began this study?
8. During this study, what is one important issue that surfaced for you?
9. What are your goals as you begin your new start?